GOD, CHURCH, ETC

GOD, CHURCH, ETC

what you need to know

JANE MAYCOCK

First published in Great Britain in 2013

Society for Promoting Christian Knowledge
36 Causton Street
London SW1P 4ST
www.spckpublishing.co.uk

British Library Cataloguing-in-Publication Data
A catalogue record for this book is available from the British Library

ISBN 978–0–281–07021–3
eBook ISBN 978–0–281–07022–0

Typeset by Graphicraft Limited, Hong Kong
First printed in Great Britain by Ashford Colour Press
Subsequently digitally printed in Great Britain

eBook by Graphicraft Limited, Hong Kong

Produced on paper from sustainable forests

for
Jonathan, Samuel, Isobel and Eleanor
with love

contents

illustrations by Dave Walker   viii
preface   ix
acknowledgements   xiii

the God stuff   1

1   names/words used to describe God   3
2   things to do with doctrines (important beliefs
    about God)   11
3   more bits about us & God   24

the Church stuff   37

4   buildings & furniture   39
5   people   47
6   stuff to do with services   58
7   events & seasons   69
8   bits that don't fit anywhere else   80

other stuff   89

9   some more things to think about   91

index of entries   111

illustrations by
Dave Walker

stroppy teenage bishop   xii

how to make church brilliant   37

the Christian festival   76

as the vicar got up to turn off the fire alarm   104

preface

why this book?

I was looking for something that I wanted to give to someone in their teens as a confirmation gift. This is the kind of book I was looking for and couldn't find.

It might not be for everyone, but it does seem that there is a gap in the market – a gap that reflects the increasingly wide gulf between what goes on inside churches, and the lives of those who live around them but rarely enter the building. It is not just that many people grow up without any knowledge of Christian faith, but that their parents, carers and teachers have very little knowledge and experience of the Church and its faith too. For many people, church is simply irrelevant. Then just occasionally something happens which briefly raises questions of what it is all about. Perhaps someone is asked to be a godparent at a Christening, or attends a funeral. Perhaps, briefly, it becomes relevant and questions are asked.

This book is not just for people in that kind of situation though. There are plenty of us who attend church services regularly who do not know why things are the way they are. Often we just accept things, or have not felt the need to ask – or perhaps we think we ought to know about something and are afraid of appearing stupid. The danger is that we become like the disciples of the teacher who tied up his cat during worship. The cat regularly walked into the meeting room and disturbed the disciples. Tying it up solved the problem. After some time, the teacher died. The disciples continued to meet, and so to tie the cat up. More time passed, and then the cat died. The disciples were concerned to follow everything that the teacher had done, so bought another cat in order to tie that one up during worship too. (Anthony de Mello tells the story in his book, *The Song of the Bird*, published in 1982.)

Losing touch with the original reason for a thing does mean that we are in danger of giving significance to things that don't matter. Conversely, we might throw out something that really does matter.

Most of us will have our own stories of misunderstanding or mishearing things. We laugh at things remembered from childhood, when our understanding is limited. Favourite examples in my family include:

- the naming of God: 'Our Father who art in heaven, Harold be thy name . . .';
- questions about the population of heaven when being taught the Lord's Prayer in traditional language: 'but there aren't any witches in heaven';
- the mystery of whether Jesus was really a reptile – 'As our Saviour tortoise, so we pray';
- and the peculiar hymn to a strangely named and unfortunate looking Teddy: 'Gladly, the cross-eyed bear . . .'

The trouble is, although we might grow out of misunderstandings like these, we might also reach adulthood without necessarily having much more to put in their place. This book is, I hope, a small contribution to increasing that understanding. We may still think Church is weird or boring, but at least we are able to say why things are the way they are, and why it is important that we believe what we do.

why a book like this?

- I didn't want a book that had to be read from the beginning to the end. I wanted something that readers could dip into, find what they want and ignore the rest. That is how internet searching tends to work, and how many people go about finding information. The internet also has a very high distraction value. Maybe, as with that, someone might begin by looking up one thing here and discover all sorts of other things too.

- It starts with the God stuff, because that is where it all begins. If God didn't matter there would be no Church. What we do in church has to come after and reflect our understanding of God.
- The 'other stuff' is there too, because the whole of life matters to God. What happens in church has to connect with the realities of life when we are not there. Christian faith permeates the whole of our lives.
- However, there is always more to know and more to be discovered. I have no illusion that this book covers everything. Most of the entries will have had whole books written on them in their own right. There are bound to be other bits that could have been included, or more that could have been said. The point though is to have something short, which – hopefully – covers some of the essentials.

All the bits in italics can easily be skipped over. However, the biblical references can be looked up and explored further if desired – perhaps with a commentary or Bible dictionary. The *name trail* is a bit of self-indulgence: I do love *words*. I am not a great scholar of Latin and Greek (although New Testament Greek was compulsory when I studied theology). I do enjoy a good detective drama on TV (as long as it is not too gory). I find that playing the detective and trailing a word to its source often gives me a richer understanding of its meaning. If this is not for you, then just ignore it!

STROPPY
TEENAGE
BISHOP

acknowledgements

Rydal Hall is a lovely place set in beautiful surroundings, and has been for me a haven of peace. My heartfelt thanks go to Jonathon Green and his team for their generosity in regularly making space for me there to think and write. Without that, this book would not be here!

I am grateful for friends and family who have encouraged me to write. Two need a special mention. Thank you Sarah, for perceptive and honest comments given at just the right time. And thank you James, for the sharing of theological thinking and insights amid parental responsibilities and the mundane tasks of family life. This comes with love and gratitude to you both.

the God stuff

'It starts with the God stuff, because that is where it all begins. If God didn't matter there would be no Church.'

1

names/words used to describe God

almighty

'Might' is strength. Being mighty means being really strong. Someone who is all-mighty is strong and powerful in all things.

Calling **God** 'almighty' should stop us in our tracks. Be warned, though: the might of God isn't always what we expect.

(see **omnipotent**)

Christ

First name 'Jesus', second name 'Christ'? No – though it looks like that. It would be better to say 'Jesus *the* Christ', because Christ means '**Messiah**'. 'Christ Jesus' is 'Messiah Jesus': not a name, but a description of who he is.

We have lots of common words that link us to Jesus in this way – like **Christmas**, **Christening** and christened, Christian and Christian name. Saying 'Messiah' in place of 'Christ' in these words helps us think again about what they mean. 'We get presents at Messiah-mas.' 'My baby cousin is going to be messiahed on Sunday.' 'I am a Messiah-person.' 'My Messiah name is Jane.'

(see **Messiah**)

Creator

Maker. **God** takes stuff and does something with it. Shapes, moulds, forms it into something useful and beautiful.

When we describe God as Creator it is not just about the beginning of the world as we know it. It says something about what God is like now: always creating. Always bringing about new possibilities. Always being the potter to our worldly clay (see *Jeremiah 18.6*). (see **creation**)

Emmanuel (also Immanuel)

Simply the Hebrew word meaning '**God** with us'. (The '-el' bit means 'God', and 'e/immanu-' means 'with us'.)

The **prophet** Isaiah speaks of a child named Immanuel, who was given as a sign that God was with the people of Judah at a difficult time (see *Isaiah 7.10–17*). In Matthew's Gospel, we read that these same words come to Joseph in a dream. In Jesus, Emmanuel, God is with us (*Matthew 1.18–23*).

Father

God is not remote. God is not just an idea. This is about a relationship: we are the child, God is the parent. Calling God 'Father' reminds us that this is real.

Of course, no human father is perfect. For some people, calling God 'father' is not helpful because they have not been able to have good relationships with their own fathers. It does say something important about God, though. God helped make us who we are. God delights in us, loves us, nurtures us, guides us, helps us.

Jesus called God 'Father'. He allowed his Father's will to be done in him. In giving up everything, the Father's life and love were displayed for everyone to see.

God

God is personal:

- the one who gave you life;
- the one you can't hide from;
- the one who loves you;
- the one who was here at the beginning;
- the one who will be here at the end.

'A god' is different. To make something 'a god' is to make it really important in your life – more important than anything else perhaps. That god will want time and attention, and maybe will get in the way of the real thing.

holy

Pure. Clean. Unspoiled. To be holy is to be set apart for **God**.

About 3,000 years ago God's people wrote down a set of laws to help them decide what was holy. This is known as the Holiness Code, and can be found in the **Bible** in the book of Leviticus. There, a whole lot of different things and activities are declared to be 'clean' or 'unclean'.

Much later, **Jesus** told his listeners that it went deeper: what is inside a person makes them clean or unclean, holy or not (*Mark 7.14–23*). Holy things don't spoil the world God has created. Holy things don't spoil relationships between people. Holy things show the world what God is like.

Holy Spirit

The Holy Spirit is God's way of being with us now. The Spirit is invisible, like the air we breathe – and like the air, we can't do without the Spirit.

Think of a flute or trumpet. It may look beautiful and shiny, but unless someone blows through it, it is silent and useless. It is the same with us. The gift of the Holy Spirit was given afresh at the **Pentecost** after Jesus' **resurrection**. Accepting the gift means that **God** can 'blow through us', and we can be useful, beautiful and fulfilled people.

Immanuel see Emmanuel

Jesus

When Mary and Joseph were told that there was a baby on the way, they were told that they had to call him Jesus (*Matthew 1.21; Luke 1.31*). Nothing else would do.

Why?

The name tells us something about who he is. It is the same as the Hebrew name Joshua. Both mean '**saviour**'. As the angel said to Joseph, 'for he will save his people from their sins'.

King

Kings reign over kingdoms. When the author of Psalm 97 declares, 'The Lord is king! Let the earth rejoice', it is clear that the Lord's kingdom is the whole earth.

Jesus starts his **ministry** by proclaiming, 'the kingdom of God has come near' – and goes on to show what he means by telling stories and healing people. **God** is the kind of king who wants people to be forgiven and whole.

When Pontius Pilate asks Jesus if he is a king, he replies, 'My kingdom is not from this world' (*John 18.36*). God's kingship is not about countries or geography. It's bigger than that. God's rule goes beyond **death** – as Jesus' **resurrection** shows.

Lamb

When John the Baptist called **Jesus** 'Lamb of God' (*John 1.29*), he wasn't thinking of cute woolly creatures of springtime, or of kebabs, or of Sunday roast. He meant the Passover lamb that played a main part in the escape of the Israelites from slavery in Egypt. **God** told them to kill a lamb and use its blood to mark the doors of their houses. The plague of death passed over these buildings, keeping the Israelites safe, ready to escape (*see Exodus 12.1–13*).

Calling Jesus 'Lamb' was a way of saying that he too would be God's way of rescuing people, and that he too would need to die to make it happen.

It's not all about **death**, though. At the end of the book of Revelation, John describes his vision of the new Jerusalem. God is at the centre of the city, and the Lamb is part of the presence of God in that place (see *Revelation 21.22–end* and *22.1–5*).

Messiah

Messiah means 'anointed one' – and that means someone special. Anointing meant putting oil on someone's head as a way of showing that they were marked out for something particular.

At the time of **Jesus**, the Jewish people were ruled by the Romans. They longed for a **Messiah** to set them free, but didn't agree on exactly what this Messiah would be like – a **King**? a **prophet**? a military leader? One thing was sure though – no one expected a Messiah like Jesus.

Yet that's what he was. Anointed by **God**, sent to turn the world inside out and to show just how far God's love can go.

omnipotent

All-powerful.

God is all-powerful, but saying so challenges our view of power. Paul repeats to the Corinthians God's words to him: 'My grace is sufficient for you, for power is made perfect in weakness' (*2 Corinthians 12.9*). The ultimate demonstration of this is in Jesus being put to **death** – and, of course, in what followed.

Name trail: omni = *Latin for 'all'; 'potent' = powerful, from the Latin* potentia.

omniscient

All-knowing.

If **God's** life is not limited by **death**, then it makes sense that God's knowing is not limited by our desire to hide things. **Jesus** reminds us that nothing is hidden from God: 'For there is nothing hidden, except to be disclosed; nor is anything secret, except to come to light' (*Mark 4.22*).

Name trail: omni = *Latin for 'all'; '-scient' from the Latin verb* scire, *meaning 'to know'.*

Redeemer

Quite a lot of our names for **God** are about God helping us get back on track, out of a bad situation and into a good one where we can thrive. 'Redeemer' is one of these. It was a familiar idea in the Roman Empire where slavery was part of life. To redeem a slave meant to pay for them to become free.

When we speak of **Jesus** as Redeemer, we mean that he has given his life so that we can be free.

(see **atonement**)

Saviour

Rescuer. One who saves.

It's like this: when **Jesus' friends** were out on the lake in a boat and a storm blew up, he was with them – asleep. They panicked, thinking they were going to drown, and woke him up. He commanded the wind and sea to be still, and saved his friends from the storm (*Mark 4.35–41*). This was just a taster: **God**'s power in Jesus that saved the **disciples** from drowning is the same power that we see in the **resurrection**.

It might not be an actual storm, but for us there may well be other times when we experience God as Saviour, coming to our rescue.

steadfast

Reliable. Something that is steadfast has got staying power. The psalms are full of confidence about **God**'s faithful, reliable, steadfast love for us.

> I declare that your steadfast love is established for ever;
> your faithfulness is as firm as the heavens.   (*Psalm 89.2*)

Trinity

Three windows overlooking the same scene might give us three different views, but it's the same scene that we look out onto through each one. It's the same with **God**. Calling God 'Trinity' is a way of pointing out that the three different views we have of God are just that – still all showing us the one God.

- We know God as **Father** – the **Creator**, originator, life-giver.
- We know God as Son – in the life of **Jesus** we see God's self-giving love.
- We know God as **Holy Spirit** – his ongoing life filling us, feeding us and helping us to grow.

Some early Christians had a word for the Trinity: *perichoresis*. It means 'round dance'. An anonymous artist pictured this as three hares chasing each other in an endless dance of love. As Christians we are caught up into that dance; into the endless delight of Father, Son and Spirit.

Another way of thinking about the Trinity is to think of a triangle. Take one of the three sides away and you no longer have a triangle. Try taking away one person of the Trinity and you find you no longer have God.

wisdom

We can think of wisdom in two ways – to do with us and to do with **God**.

When it's to do with us, it is not to do with cleverness or intelligence. We might be clever, but it won't necessarily make us any closer to God. It is not something we have or don't have. It is a gift of understanding that comes from God.

Because wisdom was understood in this way, it was seen as a way of God being present among human beings. In some writings, like the book of Proverbs (e.g. chapter 8), Wisdom is personified. Here she is God's voice calling to people to come to him.

In the New Testament, there is a strong sense that in **Jesus** this Wisdom has appeared. When Paul writes to Christians in Corinth, he declares, 'we proclaim **Christ** crucified . . . Christ the power of God and the wisdom of God' (*1 Corinthians 1.23–24*).

Word

'Word' is used of **God**, because when God speaks, things happen.

God speaks, and things come into being (*Genesis 1*).

God continues to be involved, speaking and acting in the lives of human beings. 'My word makes things happen,' says God through the **prophet** Isaiah (see *Isaiah 55.10–11*).

Yet the words of the prophets didn't seem loud enough. John describes God's powerful new beginning in **Jesus**: 'And the Word became flesh and lived among us' (*John 1.14*). Jesus is the way God speaks to us. That nailed it.

2

things to do with doctrines (important beliefs about God)

Ascension see section 7, 'events & seasons'

atonement

Great word, as it says what it means: at-one-ment.

'At-one-ment' is about mending what is broken. Healing. Making whole. **God** has reached out in **Jesus** to do the mending.

In the New Testament, the word 'atonement' is only used once (see below). Much more often, those writing use pictures to talk about what it means. There are four of these, and they all come from everyday life at the time of Jesus.

1 *Expiation* – an image from the Temple **worship**: God wipes away **sin**, just as he had through people bringing the **sacrifices** set out in the laws of Moses. 'In this is love, not that we loved God but that he loved us and sent his Son to be the atoning sacrifice for our sins' (*1 John 4.10*).

2 *Redemption* – an image from the slave markets of the Roman Empire: redeeming a slave means paying for him or her to be free, so God has paid for us to be free. 'For freedom **Christ** has set us free. Stand firm, therefore, and do not submit again to a yoke of slavery' (*Galatians 5.1*).

3 *Reconciliation* – an image from the world of conflict and war: reconciliation means bringing about peace so there's no more fighting between different sides. Through Jesus, 'God was pleased

to reconcile to himself all things . . . by making peace through the blood of his cross' (*Colossians 1.20*).

4 *Justification* – an image from the law courts: the person in the dock is acquitted, declared innocent of the thing that they were accused of. Similarly, God justifies us, says were are ok, and gives us a new start: 'we know that a person is justified not by the works of the law but through faith in Jesus Christ' (*Galatians 2.16*).

God brings about this 'at-one-ment' through Jesus' **death** and **resurrection**. He shows us how far his love can reach, and the fresh start that is offered to every one of us.

Fascinating fact: the word translated as 'atonement' in Romans 3.24 is hilasterion, *which means 'mercy seat'. The mercy seat was part of the Ark of the Covenant. It was the place from which God spoke to his people. (See Exodus 25.17–22 for the instructions he gave to Moses.) When the Temple was built, the mercy seat was located in the Holy of Holies. It was the place where atonement was effected. The priests only went into the Holy of Holies once a year – on the Day of Atonement (see Leviticus 16).*

Bible

Anger, conflict, **sex**, murder, complaining, outspokenness, family sagas, infighting, power struggles, reconciliation, advice, **prayers**, lament, promises, extraordinary events, mad men, drunkenness, heroines, heroes and more. The Bible's got nice bits and tough stuff – all the stuff you'd expect when **God** and human beings inhabit the same space.

- It's more of a library than a single book. It's got letters, history, poetry, legal stuff and more. Its 66 books are divided into two main sections: the Old Testament (39) and the New Testament (27).

- Another word for 'Testament' is '**covenant**'. It means 'agreement' – an agreement between God and human beings.
- Old Testament: often called the Hebrew Bible, because it was mostly written in Hebrew, and is still the Bible of the Jewish people. Its writings date from as early as 1000 BC to about 250 BC. Christians have called it 'old' because they wanted to distinguish it from the 'new' writings which are to do with **Jesus** and the beginnings of Christianity.
- New Testament: writings that are about Jesus and what happened to some of his followers after he died.
- Sometimes it's all referred to as '**Scripture**', which just means 'writings'.

Christmas see section 7, 'events & seasons' and incarnation

covenant

An agreement or promise between two parties. In the book of Genesis we hear of **God** making a covenant with Noah after the flood (*Genesis 9.8–17*). A bit later the covenant with Abram is described (*Genesis 15.18*). Particularly important for the Israelites was the Sinai covenant. God called Moses up Mount Sinai and gave him the Ten Commandments – and more (*from Exodus 19.20 to the end of chapter 31*). This 'law' became known as Torah and remains the basis of Jewish **faith** today.

In English, another word meaning the same is 'testament' (see **Bible**). The use of 'old' and 'new' is to show that God has made a new agreement with people through **Jesus**. This covenant was spoken of by the **prophet** Jeremiah: 'I will be their God, and they shall be my people' (see *Jeremiah 31.31–34*).

creation

God made the world.

Billions of years. Millions of stars in countless galaxies. One planet earth. Oceans, deserts, savannahs, rivers, mountains, snow, rainforest, fields, penguins, tree frogs, beetles, bears, fur, scales, skin cells, and microscopic particles that have never been seen. Vast, intricate and extraordinary: God is responsible for all this.

There are two creation stories at the beginning of the **Bible**. They are not descriptions of how it happened – after all, they describe different things. They both say very important things about God and creation:

- God is a god who brings order out of chaos (*Genesis 1.1—2.3*).
- God declared that the created world was very good (*Genesis 1.31*).
- People are made in God's image (*Genesis 1.27*).
- God formed people, into whom he breathes life (*Genesis 2.7*).
- God sees that people need companions (*Genesis 2.18*).
- God charges people to look after creation (*Genesis 2.15*).

Saying that God created the world also means this: God goes on creating, sustaining and renewing the whole created world. We human beings might not be perfect, but God wants us to look after the world with him.

(see **creator**)

cross

Talking of 'the cross' is a shorthand way of talking about **Jesus' death** and what is achieved.

(see **atonement**)

crucifixion

A common form of execution in the Roman Empire. Like others, **Jesus** was made to carry the cross piece to the place of execution.

Here his hands were nailed onto it and the whole thing fixed to the upright post. It was a particularly slow and horrible way to die, saved for the worst criminals.

Name trail: it quite literally means 'fixing to a cross', and comes from two Latin words – cruci meaning 'cross' and figere, 'to fix'.

Easter see section 7, 'events & seasons' and resurrection

eternity/eternal life

Our lives and what we do are limited by time. There's only so much we can fit in. We haven't time to tidy bedrooms or empty the dishwasher – we want to do other things with 'our time'. Our lives are measured by time. Term times and holidays. Celebrations for birthdays and how long people have been married. When a person dies, we celebrate or lament how old they were.

Eternity is about there being more to life than what happens as we go on day by day. It's about the life **God** gives being bigger than the human life we experience now. It's about a quality of life we can begin to discover now, through **Jesus**, but we'll meet it more fully when we die.

Note: this is not to be confused with the idea of everlasting life, which means going on for ever through time.

glory

If someone's said to be 'basking in glory' it means they are a bit of a celebrity, at least for that moment. They've got fame. People recognize them in the street. 'Reflected glory' means that if you are close to them in some way, a bit of that rubs off on you. A glorious building is one that is splendid or magnificent.

When we talk of the glory of **God** we mean the same, and more. When biblical writers describe appearances of God to people, they often describe splendour or light. When God's around, the light is so bright you have to shield your eyes – unless you are Moses. (See *Exodus 24.16–17 and chapter 34.29;* also **Transfiguration**.)

grace

Favour. Goodwill. A gift of **God**, given to human beings.

When Gabriel visits Mary with the extraordinary news that she is to be the mother of **Jesus**, he says, 'Greetings, favoured one! The Lord is with you.' 'Favoured one' is also translated sometimes as 'full of grace'. And that says it all really: grace is about being favoured by God. The gift is that he is with us.

Every letter in the New Testament from Paul includes in the greeting a **prayer** for grace. Most often he writes, 'Grace to you and peace from God our **Father** and the Lord Jesus **Christ**'. He reminds us that grace is something that comes to us from God through Jesus, whose life is itself an expression of God's grace.

heaven

Heaven is real. We often say we'll go there when we die. But what do we mean? We won't find it on a map and we don't know what it will look like.

For hundreds of years people have used picture language to describe the kind of thing we expect of heaven. Fluffy white clouds, pearly gates, harps and angels might not appeal to each one of us, but they are all ways of saying that heaven is something beautiful, precious and beyond earthly life.

In the **Bible**, the books of Psalms, Job, Isaiah, Ezekiel, Daniel and Revelation all give us glimpses of heaven. We see a court with a throne, angelic beings and heavenly **worship**. We also see archangels involved in the business of the earth – and that speaks volumes. When Jesus teaches his followers about the kingdom of heaven, it is not about something entirely separate from the earth. It is to do with the presence of **God** in the midst of human life – even if we are not always aware of it.

Heaven is a reality that we *can* experience here and now; but whatever it is like, we will know it more fully when this life is over. (see **eternity/eternal life**)

hell

As with **heaven**, people have always used pictures to try and say what we mean by hell. **Jesus** gives such a picture in his parable of the rich man and Lazarus (*Luke 16.19–31*). Imagery may include fire, darkness, gloom, lakes of sulphur, demons, torments and the **devil**. It may not be a place on a map, but talk of hell says some important things:

- the way we live now matters to **God**;
- the way we live now makes a difference to what happens when we die;
- hell is to do with punishment as a consequence of how we behave now;
- it is about separation from God.

So, talk of hell reminds us that how we live our lives here and now matters. *But*, there are two things to remember:

1 It's no good speaking confidently about eternal fires and so on. This is picture language for something we don't have information about. Who knows what it might be like?
2 It is no one's business to say who is 'going to hell' except God's. Human beings, thankfully, don't make this decision.

(see **judgement**)

incarnation

This describes **Jesus** – **God** becoming fully human.

Sometimes the human aspect of Jesus seems most obvious: being born as a baby in a stable; feeling tiredness, hunger and thirst (*John 4.1–8*); struggling with God's will (*Mark 14.32–36*); feeling abandoned (*Mark 15.34*).

Sometimes the 'God-ness' of Jesus shines through: as he heals people; in the events we call **miracles**; and most of all in the **resurrection**.

The event of the incarnation – Jesus' birth – is what we celebrate at **Christmas**.

Name trail: from the Latin incarnare: *the 'carn-' bit is from the word for flesh,* carnis, *so 'in-carn-ation' means to become flesh.*

judgement

Making a judgement is like making a decision. Is a thing good or bad? Is it well done or poorly done? We make judgements about ourselves and other people all the time.

Sometimes we have bad experiences of being judged by others, and this can cloud our sense of what it means to say that **God** is Judge. What does it mean to say Christians believe in judgement?

- God does judge us. He's given us guidelines about how to behave towards other people, the created world and God himself. It's natural to think that he'd like us to do our best to live up to what he intends.
- However, it's not like waiting to hear if we've passed an exam, because . . .
- . . . God loves us, which makes judgement feel rather less worrying.
- In John's Gospel **Jesus** says, 'I do not judge anyone who hears my words and does not keep them, for I came not to judge the world, but to save the world' (*John 12.47*).
- The Christian tradition is of belief in the 'last judgement' – something that happens in the future at the **second coming** (see Jesus' **parable** in *Matthew 25.31–46*).

mercy

The quality of compassion or forgiveness. Mercy is evident in a relationship between people. It is shown to someone who is powerless, from someone who is in a position of power or authority over them.

miracles

The Israelites crossing the Red Sea (*Exodus 14.21–23*). The sun being held back for Joshua (*Joshua 10.12–14*). The endless supply of oil and meal for Elijah and the widow of Zarephath (*1 Kings 17.8–16*). Elisha bringing to life the son of the Shunammite woman (*2 Kings 4.32–37*). **Jesus** walking on water, turning water into wine, feeding 5,000 people, calming a storm. Jesus performing unexplained and extraordinary healing – many times.

All these are called miracles: things that seem to be impossible within the laws of nature.

Some people try to find a rational explanation for these things, or say that they didn't really happen as described. However:

- if **God** is God, **almighty** and all of that, then he is certainly able to make such things happen. So the question is not so much *if* it happened, but *why* it did.
- the laws of nature are not as deterministic as some people once thought. The way the world is made allows for new and surprising things to happen.
- in his Gospel, John doesn't use the word 'miracle'. He calls these extraordinary events 'signs'. These things are about helping us to notice what we are often too busy to see: God is at work, with us, in us, around us.

nativity

The nativity is the birth of **Jesus**.
(see **Christmas, incarnation**)

Name trail: from the Latin word nativitas, *which simply means 'birth'.*

resurrection

The resurrection is what happened to **Jesus**: killed on the Friday and buried, but seen alive on the Sunday. There he was: no ghost, but a living, breathing, eating human being with the marks of his wounds still showing.

Belief in the resurrection is central to Christian **faith**. Before Jesus, the Jews believed that when a person died they went to a shadowy grey sort of place called Sheol, and basically that was it. Some thought there would be a general resurrection 'at the last day,' when **God** would raise everyone – whenever that might be. Some Greeks believed that everyone had a **soul**, which was 'trapped' inside a **body**. When the body died, the soul went on to exist in a different way. Others thought that there was simply nothing more.

But here was Jesus, showing us something different. Jesus' resurrection shows us that Sheol/**death** could not keep him, because the life and love of God is bigger and stronger. Jesus was the same person as before, yet had come through death. His resurrection demonstrates God's creative power. We live in the light of what happened to Jesus.

righteousness

Nowadays the word 'righteousness' sounds a bit old-fashioned. We don't hear people being called 'righteous'. However, there's *lots* of talk about 'rights'. These things are closely linked, but to see the difference we can think of them as being to do with the outside and inside of a person.

'Rights' are often more about what's on the outside of a person. When I talk about 'my rights' it's to do with how I'm treated by other people or organizations. We have a strong sense of fairness and 'rights' from a very early age.

'Righteousness' is more about what is on the inside of a person. It is about how what is inside comes out in the way someone lives.

God is described as righteous. It's a way of saying that all God's essential goodness and 'rightness' and fairness is expressed in the way he acts. In his letter to the Romans, Paul says that in the gospel, 'the righteousness of God is revealed' (*Romans 1.16–17*). God's righteous action is seen in the life, **death** and **resurrection** of **Jesus**. We are caught up in this. Our openness to God means that God can make us righteous too.

sacrament

A sacrament is one of the ways people come to **God**. There are two main sacraments: **Baptism** and **Holy Communion**. Both of these involve not just our minds, but certain actions too – being washed, or receiving **bread** and **wine**. We enter into what the actions mean.

It's not just about what we do, though; it's about what God does too. Sometimes a sacrament is said to be 'an outward and visible sign of an inward and spiritual grace' (a description that probably goes back to St Augustine, who lived about 1,600 years ago). Sacraments are signs of God's **grace** – of God at work invisibly in us.

Baptism and Holy Communion are often called 'dominical sacraments', because **Jesus** himself instructed his **disciples** to go on doing them (see *1 Corinthians 11.23–26* and *Matthew 28.19*). The Roman Catholic Church recognizes five other sacraments too: **confirmation**, **penance**, **marriage**, **ordination** and the last rites (also called extreme unction).

Name trail: 'dominical' means 'to do with the Lord' as it comes from dominus, *the Latin word for 'Lord'. 'sacrament' comes from the Latin* sacer – *something that is **holy**.*

sacrifice

Giving up something precious of your own in order to put things right – that is making a sacrifice.

21

Jesus and his Jewish **friends** grew up with the very thorough system of sacrifices that **God** had given the Jews as part of the **covenant**. Sacrifices were performed in the Temple in Jerusalem. They were about being purified from **sin**, and being right with God. Jesus' parents took him to the Temple when he was a baby, and offered sacrifices 'according to the law of Moses' (*Luke 2.22–24*).

Jesus himself is described as a sacrifice. The writer to the Hebrews uses the image of sacrifice a lot to talk about Jesus' **death**. It was to make us pure (*Hebrews 9.13–14*), but goes further than the old sacrifices could. His **resurrection** demonstrates the new life that God gives.

salvation

It's about being saved. You have to be saved *from* something – from something bad happening, a threat, something that might hurt, or a bad situation.

Salvation might be the act of a **friend**. 'Help me with my home-work and you'll save me from being in trouble at school.' 'Let me stay over at your place and you'll save me from my parents seeing me like this.'

You might find yourself saying to someone who helps you out of a mess and into a good place, 'You're my salvation!'

God can go deeper still. Sometimes my worst enemy is myself. God helps us with those bits of ourselves that we don't like or we've let go bad. We don't have to be overwhelmed by them, but can turn them into something good. God saves us from all sorts of things. God is our salvation.

Scripture

The word simply means 'writing', *but* – it's often used to indicate that a particular set of writings are thought of as **holy**. Because they are holy, they have **authority**. This means I accept that I can learn from these writings – about **God**, about the ways of God in the world, about myself and about how to live.

The Old Testament on its own is known as the Hebrew Scriptures. The **Bible** as a whole is sometimes called 'Holy Scripture'.

second coming

'**Christ** has died, Christ is risen, Christ will come again': words declared by thousands of people each week in the Communion service. And that says it all really. The **creator God** who has shown his love in coming to us in **Jesus**, will one day 'sort the world out' with something completely new. It is a belief rooted in our understanding that we live in a relationship with God, Creator and **Saviour**.

This newness is already seen in the **resurrection** of Jesus. Paul uses a harvesting image and calls Jesus 'the first fruits' – in other words, there's more to come (*1 Corinthians 15.20*). Isaiah speaks of deserts blossoming, of levelled ground and preying animals living peacefully with their victims (*Isaiah 11.6–9* and *chapter 35*). John gives us a picture of a new **heaven** and earth, free of pain and lit by the presence of God (*Revelation 21*). We don't know when, where or exactly what, but it will be good.

3

more bits about us & God

apostle

Jesus' closest companions, the twelve apostles. Do we think of them in stained-glass windows or old paintings, with **halos**, flowing robes and wise faces? Or do we with think of them with dusty feet and sweaty bodies, hauling fishing boats on to the shore, receiving abuse for working as the Romans' tax collector, or hurling abuse and plotting ways to get rid of these foreign rulers?

Jesus did not choose his apostles because they were obviously special in some way. They were ordinary. They didn't fully understand what he was about. But they stuck with him, and for the most part they did what he asked them to do. Apostles had to be people of action.

Apostle Paul was a bit of an action man too – as passionate about doing the work of Jesus as he had been about trying to kill off his followers.

All the apostles have one thing in common: they meet the risen Jesus and feel different. How else could those who fled the **crucifixion** and hid behind locked doors have become the leaders of the emerging Christian **Church**?

Name trail: this comes directly from the Greek word apostellein, *which means 'to send out'. An 'apostle' is someone who is sent out, a messenger.*

blessing

God gives these words to Moses for Aaron and the priests to use:

The LORD bless you and keep you;
the LORD make his face to shine upon you, and be gracious to you;
the LORD lift up his countenance upon you, and give you peace.
(Numbers 6.24–26)

It's a bit like being greeted by someone with a beaming smile on their face. That smile makes it clear that they are pleased to see you and want the best for you. Church services nearly always end with a **blessing**. We leave knowing that **God** is with us.

Body of Christ

Another word for the **Church** – not a particular denomination, but *all* Christians.

When Paul writes to Christians in Corinth, he has to deal with the fact that within the church there were divisions. People disagreed about what was right, and they claimed the **authority** of different people to back up their arguments (*1 Corinthians 3.1–4*). He helps them to see that they are all important – just as different parts of the **body** each have their own job to do. He explains this image in the whole of 1 Corinthians 12. He also uses it in his letter to the Romans (*Romans 12.4–8*), and in Ephesians (*Ephesians 4.4–16*).

It's an image that has stuck. We are all different, but we all belong to the same **faith**. We are all part of the Body of Christ, of which **Jesus** is the head.

devil

Opponent of **God**. Resident of **hell**. In **Jesus' parable** of final **judgement**, the king in the story sends those who did nothing for the needy 'into the eternal fire prepared for the devil and his angels' (*Matthew 25.31–46*). There are similar images in the book of Revelation. As time went on, the figure of a devil with cloven hoofs, horns and a pointy tail develops in Christian art and gets into popular imagination.

This kind of image of the devil leaping about and trying to get at people with a red-hot poker might belong more to cartoons than the **Bible**. Even so, it does remind us of something important: there is a clear understanding in Christianity of evil, which is opposed to the desires of God for people.

(see also **Satan**)

Name trail: 'devil' is an English word, which we use to translate the Greek diabolos, *which the Greeks used for a Hebrew word, 'Satan'.*

disciple

Someone who follows **Jesus** and learns from him. The twelve **apostles** are also known as disciples, but there are lots of other disciples too. Jesus expects his disciples to put into practice what they learn (e.g. *Luke 10*).

Jesus has lots of disciples here and now. Disciples are not people who have somehow 'made it', but are people who are going on learning. Every Christian person is a disciple, learning from Jesus and putting it into practice.

Name trail: disciple means 'one who learns'. It comes directly from the Latin word, discipulus, *which was widely used for a scholar or pupil. When the New Testament was translated from Greek into Latin,* discipulus *was used for the Greek,* mathetes, *which also means, 'someone who learns'.*

fasting

Normally this means not eating for a time in order to achieve something which is not about food itself. It's a way of getting closer to **God**.

If I give up chocolate in Lent because I want to lose weight, then I'm not really fasting. If I deny myself chocolate in Lent because I want to be reminded about not taking good things for granted, and because I want to focus more on God who provides all our food, then I am fasting.

Fasting is not just about *not* doing something. It is about doing something more. When I would normally eat, I will pray instead. If I give up a luxury like sweets or alcohol, I will give the money I would have spent to a charity instead.

Jesus did it (*Matthew 4.2*) and taught about it (*Matthew 6.16–18*).

hope

It can seem a bit 'airy-fairy': 'I hope I win a million pounds/a luxury holiday/that brand new computer' – or whatever you daydream about. But that's not hope. Hope is not vague wishful thinking about the future. Hope is solid. And specific.

Peter writes that **Jesus** 'has given us a new birth into a living hope through the **resurrection** of Jesus Christ from the dead, and into an inheritance that is imperishable, undefiled, and un-fading, kept in **heaven** for you . . .' (*1 Peter 1.3–4*). Christian hope is both something we do and something we have. What we *have* is the knowledge that **God** raised Jesus from **death** and gave him new life. What we *do* is live expecting that God will do this for us too.

listening

Friendships are no good if all we ever do is talk at our **friends**; we have to listen to them too. If they are good friends then we value what they have to say. It's the same with **God**. It's no good just talking at God – he wants us to listen to him too.

It sounds great doesn't it? However:

- we don't often hear God in a straightforward kind of way, and we're not the only ones. Samuel needed someone to tell him that is was God's voice he was hearing (*1 Samuel 3.1–18*).

- and Balaam needed to realize that God was speaking to him through someone else. (In his case, his donkey. See *Numbers 22.22–35*.)
- sometimes God speaks and no one is listening. In Isaiah, God's servant has to demand attention: 'listen to me . . . pay attention, you peoples . . . !' (*Isaiah 49*).
- there are lots of distractions and it's hard to listen. Sometimes when we do try and listen to God we can't hear because of the chatter in our own heads.
- sometimes we are fearful and think 'I'm not going to listen because I know what you're going to say!' The trouble is it might not be what we expect, and maybe we miss out on something good.

(see also **prayer** and **guidance**)

martyr

A person who gives up something precious – usually their life – for something they believe in. Lots of people have died rather than deny their Christian **faith**: Dietrich Bonhoeffer (Germany, 1945), Wang Zhiming (China, 1973), Oscar Romero (El Salvador, 1980). It goes on happening.

Name trail: 'martyr' comes directly from the Greek word martus, *which means 'witness'.*

parable

A story that invites us to think about something in a different way. **Jesus** used parables a lot, some very short and others longer. He told stories of everyday life. He got everyone's attention by talking about what was familiar – then he'd make something strange or scandalous happen so people would sit up and think. A businessman who sells everything just to own one pearl? A farmer who is so careless as to let seed fall on rocks and thorns? A Samaritan who helps a Jew? Hired labourers who are paid the same for one hour's work as those who did a whole day? A **father** who runs out to welcome the son who has treated him abominably? What *is* Jesus on about?

And that's the point: we have to listen, get our heads inside the story and work it out.

penance

A penance is something a person has to do in order to show that they are sorry for something they have done. If a person confesses to a **priest** something that they have done wrong, the priest can declare that **God** forgives them. The priest might also suggest something for the person to do to demonstrate that they are sorry. It might be to do with **prayer**, or it might be an action. Whatever it is, it shows on the outside that, inside, the person is sorry for what they have done.

penitence, penitent

To be penitent is to feel sorry about something you have done. Penitence is the state of being sorry. Both words include the idea of doing something to show that you are sorry.

prayer

Talking to **God**. Listening to God. Being with God. Giving God a chance to talk to us.

It's not quite the same as having your best **friend** sitting next to you, though. How do we do it, and where?

Find a good place and time, maybe:

- in your bedroom/the garden shed/the bathroom because it's the only place you get to be alone/when you're out walking;
- first thing in the morning – ask God to be with you in the business of the day;
- last thing at night – tell God what's been going on;
- in **church**, at a service with other people;
- in church, when it's quiet and no one's around.

We can pray in different ways:

- just talk – tell God what's on your mind;
- use prayers that someone else has written;
- look at a bit of the **Bible** and focus on that (what's in the story? who says what? what can I learn about myself and God?);
- focus on something **Jesus** says or does;
- use the words of a chorus or **hymn**;
- sit in silence, open to God.

The main thing is keeping in touch.
(see also **listening, prayers, guidance**)

prophet/prophecy

A prophet is someone who speaks God's word. Through a prophet we hear what **God** thinks about a situation. A prophecy is what they say.

We might think that a prophet is someone who predicts what is going to happen in the future. Occasionally this is true, but it's much more than that. In the Bible prophets are always in the business of trying to call people back to God and behave as God wants them to.

repent/repentance

To repent is to be sorry for something you have done. Repentance is the act of being sorry.

In the New Testament, the call for people to repent is part of the preaching of John the Baptist and **Jesus** (for example, *Mark 1.4, 15*). Repentance is about accepting the presence and rule of **God**.

Name trail: in the New Testament the Greek word used is metanoia, *which translates literally as 'change of mind'. However, the way it is used implies that it is not just about what goes on in the head, but involves a wholehearted turning or change of direction.*

revere/reverent

To revere something is to look up to or respect something that is considered special or **holy**. Being reverent is showing this in the way you act.

saint

A **holy** person whose life shows that they have stood up for **God**. We can read stories of saints doing amazing things. We hear of the remains of saints seeming to cause **miracles** after they have died. We see pictures of them with **halos** round their heads. It can all seem very different from us.

But – if you look at Paul's letters in the New Testament, he frequently addresses them 'to the saints in . . .', or to the people 'called to be saints . . .'. These were ordinary people, just like you and me. It's clear from what he writes that there were plenty of people in the churches not behaving as we might think a saint should behave. But Paul knows that all of us are called by God to be part of the **Church**. That's what a saint is: you and me, called by God to show his love and light in the way we live. Holy people.

Satan

At the start of the book of Job, Satan and **God** have a conversation. God provokes Satan, and Satan accuses God. God allows Satan to do some bad stuff to Job and his family, to see if Job will turn his back on God (which he doesn't). It points us to some important things about Satan:

- his name means Accuser – and that's what he is and does;
- Satan goes about on earth (there's no mention of **hell**);
- God allows Satan to do what he does;
- God knows that Job is free to turn against him.

In addition:

- he works among human beings to provoke them to go against God: for example, David in *1 Chronicles 21.1*, Peter in *Matthew 16.23* and Judas in *Luke 22.3*. (He's mentioned by name 14 times.)
- **Jesus** sees the work of Satan in any person or situation that goes against the purposes of God for healing and wholeness (for example, *Matthew 4.10*; *Luke 10.18*; and *Luke 13.16*).

(see **devil**)

sin

Imagine using a bow and arrow to hit the centre mark on a target. You shoot, but it misses the mark. This is how people writing at the time of **Jesus** thought about sin: they used a word from archery that meant 'to miss the mark'.

Sin is about what hurts ourselves and other people. Most of us know what is good, and what is bad and harmful, and we could probably spend ages listing individual wrongs that people do. Sometimes it is good to think of specific things like this. But it is also helpful to think about 'sin' rather than 'sins'. When Paul writes to Christians in Rome he reminds them that 'all have sinned and fall short of the glory of God' (*Romans 3.23*).

It begs a question, though: if **God** has got such high standards, why didn't he just make us perfect? Well:

- if he had done this, we'd be like robots;
- God has made us much more wonderful – with minds to think and make decisions;
- our own interests and God's interests don't always match, and we have to choose.

God loves us. He wants us to choose the best way and helps us to do this. Paul goes on to say that sinners 'are now justified by his **grace** as a gift, through the redemption that is in **Christ** Jesus . . .' (*Romans 3.24*).

(see **confession**)

soul

This is the word we use to describe the bit of us that goes on after **death**. Here are the problems with it.

- The Hebrews didn't have an idea of 'soul'; they talked about 'life'. The Hebrew word is *nephesh*. It means 'breath' or 'life', and so sometimes was used to talk about the self – 'the living, breathing me'.
- Some Greek thinkers used 'body' to describe 'my physical **body**, the bit that dies', and 'soul' to describe 'the bit that doesn't die but carries on'.
- When **Jesus** was around, people disagreed about what happened when they died. For example, the Sadducees didn't believe in resurrection and tried to trick Jesus with their question (see *Luke 20.27–33*).
- People still disagree about it now.

Even so, there is something about every person which we call 'me'. I don't look like I did when I was a baby. I may not look much like I did last year. I may change my hair cut and colour, but I am still me. The cells in my body grow, change, die and are replaced, but I am still me.

'Soul' is the word we use to describe this essential me – the inner conviction of who I am, that cannot be destroyed.

spiritual gifts

You might have a natural talent for sport or maths or making things. Natural talents are really important, but are different from spiritual gifts.

These are things in people that show that the **Holy Spirit** is at work in the **church** community as a whole. Paul talks about a church being like a **body**, where all the parts are important – eyes, legs, toes, hands, kidneys, and so on. In the same way, everyone's gifts are needed to make the whole body work properly. Paul mentions gifts of **wisdom**, knowledge, **faith**, healing, working **miracles**, **prophecy**, discernment, teaching, exhortation, apostleship, evangelism, generosity, leadership, speaking in tongues and interpretation of tongues. It's no good anyone boasting about what they can do. All are important, and all come from **God**. (See *Romans 12.4–8*; *1 Corinthians 12*; *Ephesians 4.1–16*.)

suffering

Something bad happens and we ask, 'Where was **God** then?' 'Why is the person I love ill?' 'Why did so many people die?' 'Why is there so much famine?'

Sometimes we can answer these questions. A bad thing happens because of the evil, thoughtless or selfish action of another person. Sometimes things happen for no obvious reason, with no obvious answer.

What the Christian **faith** does say is this: God is in it with us. We see this in what happened to **Jesus**. Like us, he did not want to suffer. He wrestled with God's will. He prayed that what he saw coming would not have to happen. It did.

Jesus died, but what then happened shows us that **death** does not have the last word. Whatever suffering we experience or see in others now, God is there too. God knows what it is like. God helps us through it. God's gifts of life and love have the last word.

wrath

Another word for anger. 'The wrath of **God**' is a notion that has been used by some Christians to make others feel beaten down by a sense of their own inadequacy. Surely, God must be angry with them.

God does get angry – with injustice, and with those who blatantly go against his good will for the world. But he'll never turn away anyone who says sorry.

the Church stuff

'What we do in church has to come after and reflect our under-standing of God.'

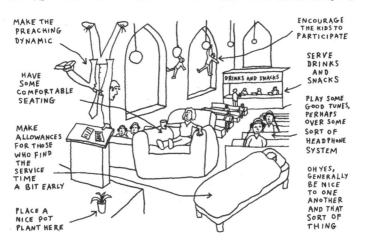

HOW TO MAKE CHURCH BRILLIANT

MAKE THE PREACHING DYNAMIC

HAVE SOME COMFORTABLE SEATING

MAKE ALLOWANCES FOR THOSE WHO FIND THE SERVICE TIME A BIT EARLY

PLACE A NICE POT PLANT HERE

ENCOURAGE THE KIDS TO PARTICIPATE

SERVE DRINKS AND SNACKS

DRINKS AND SNACKS

PLAY SOME GOOD TUNES, PERHAPS OVER SOME SORT OF HEADPHONE SYSTEM

OH YES, GENERALLY BE NICE TO ONE ANOTHER AND THAT SORT OF THING

4

buildings & furniture

altar

A kind of table where the **bread** and **wine** are placed during **Holy Communion**. Why this name? Well:

- Christianity grew out of the Jewish **faith**;
- for the Jews an altar was important as the place where a **sacrifice** was made to **God**;
- keeping this name is a reminder of the sacrificial love of **God**;
- God's love is at the heart of a communion service: God gave himself for us, so that we can live in his love. As John wrote not long after **Jesus' death** and **resurrection**, 'In this is love, not that we loved God but that he loved us and sent his Son to be the atoning sacrifice for our **sins**' (*1 John 4.10*).

(see also **communion table, Holy Communion** and **sacrifice**)

baptistery

The part of a **church** building where baptisms happen.

In some churches this is where the **font** is.

In churches where adult **baptism** by full immersion is usual, the baptistery may look like a small swimming pool. The pool will be big enough for two adults, one being immersed and one performing the ceremony. This is often hidden under the floor, but can be opened up when needed.

Occasionally the baptistery is a separate building close to the main door of the church or **cathedral**. This symbolizes the fact that baptism is the way into the Christian **faith**.

candles

Churches can be full of candles – or have none at all. Two candles on the **altar**. Candles either side of the **cross** in a **procession**. **Baptism** candles. A **paschal** candle on **Easter** Day. A **prayer** stand with opportunities for people to light a candle (sometimes called votive candles).

A few hundred years ago candles were the main source of light in an often dark building. But lots of candles were a sign of wealth. At the **Reformation** some churches wanted to get back to a simpler form of **worship**. Some **church** reformers did not want people's attention to be drawn to an object like a cross or **crucifix**. The number of candles were reduced. Church services happened in daylight hours. Candles were no longer needed to provide light.

So why do we still have them?

- Candles are symbols of the light of **God** shining among us.
- They remind us of all the images of light in the **Bible**.
- **Jesus** tells his **disciples**, 'You are the light of the world ... let your light shine before others ...' (*Matthew 5.14, 16*).
- Above all, Jesus describes himself saying, 'I am the light of the world. Whoever follows me will never walk in darkness but will have the light of life' (*John 8.12*).

cathedral

A cathedral is the **church** where the **bishop**'s 'throne' or seat is – because *cathedra* in Greek means 'seat'. As bishops oversee large areas of a country called dioceses, the cathedral is the principal church for a **diocese**. Some people on the staff of a cathedral will just work there. Others based at the cathedral will have work that is to do with the whole diocese.

chancel

In a traditional **church** building, this is the part of the church in front of where the **congregation** are sitting. Often, the chancel is where the **choir** sits, and the **altar** or **communion table** is beyond that.

If you go back to before the **Reformation**, the chancel was the place in the church that was reserved for the **priest**s. All the other people coming to communion watched from a distance – not good, given that communion is all about **God**'s welcome!

chapel

A place of **worship** that has an **altar** or **communion table** in it, but that is usually smaller than a **church**. A chapel can be a small room within a church building, or part of a different building altogether – inside a college, hospital, school, prison or even a private house.

In some places, 'chapel' meant the place of Christian worship that wasn't the Anglican church – perhaps Methodist, Baptist or Free Church. People would describe themselves as being 'church' or 'chapel'.

(see also **denomination**)

Fascinating fact: 'chapel' originally meant 'cloak' – not just any old cloak but the one that belonged to St Martin, the Roman soldier who cut his cloak in half and gave half to a beggar. This cloak was called a cappella. *It was kept as a **holy** relic, taken by kings into battle and eventually given its own place of safe keeping. This place was simply called the 'cappella' or 'chapel', and here it was looked after by* cappellani, *or '**chaplains**'.*

church

The word 'church' has two meanings. The most important one is this:

• people gathered together to **worship God**.

From this, it has also come to mean:

• a building where Christians come to worship God.

A church is a building with certain things inside – an **altar, pews** or chairs in rows; an organ, **minister**s wearing robes, and so on. It is a building in which certain things happen – **baptism**s, sometimes **weddings** and **funeral**s.

Sometimes it seems as if this second meaning matters most – yet the Church would still be here without the building.
(see also section 5, 'people')

Name trail: 'church' comes from the Greek word kuriakon, *which means 'the Lord's'. It was a shorthand way of saying 'the house of the Lord'. This also gives us the word 'kirk', which is commonly used in Scotland to refer to the Church of Scotland or Free Church.*

communion table

The table on which the **bread** and **wine** are placed during a service of **Holy Communion**. It is the same piece of furniture that some Christians call the **altar**, but with a different emphasis. When Christians use the words 'communion table' they usually want to avoid the idea of **sacrifice** that comes with the word 'altar'. Instead, they emphasize the meal **Jesus** had with his **friends** before he died. He shared bread and wine with them, saying that these things were his **body** and blood. We call this meal the Last Supper, or **Lord's Supper**.

cross

A symbol – an image that says something about Christianity.

- The Romans put **Jesus** to death by crucifying him – nailing him to a cross.
- The empty cross tells us of Jesus' **death**, but also that **God** raised him to new life.
- The cross proclaims the love God has shown in and through Jesus.

- It is a reminder of how we should live: sharing in the life of God, demonstrating self-giving love in the world around us.
- People declare this in lots of ways – in their jewellery, on car bumper stickers, a cross hung on the wall of a home, even in the shape of **church** buildings.

crucifix

A **cross** with the figure of **Jesus** on it. A symbol of Jesus crucified. Some people find it a bit gruesome, or think it tells only half the story, but it is a reminder of how much Jesus suffered for us. He gave his life.

font

The bowl that contains the water at a **baptism**. It can be small, brought out when needed to stand on a table. It can be set in its own stand. It can be like a large sink with a plug hole in the bottom, set in stone, with or without a lid.

A font might not look like anything special, but the name reminds us of what it contains: 'font' comes from a Latin word meaning fountain – fresh, running water, continuously bubbling up from its source. That's what the love of **God** is like: always bubbling up and running over; cleansing, refreshing, life-giving.

lectern

A bookstand – but not any old bookstand for any old book. Churches often have a special place for the **Bible** to show that it is important. The lectern is this place. Public Bible reading during a service happens here at the lectern. (It's practical too. Bibles used in public **worship** are often big books that need a stand so that the readers don't have to be weight-lifters too.)

Sometimes the lectern is made to look like an eagle – the living creature that represents John's Gospel. An eagle has such sharp eyes that even from great heights it can see the detail of the land below – and John is often thought of as a 'bird's-eye view' of the gospel. When the lectern looks like an eagle we are reminded that through the Bible we find a different way of looking at life.

nave

The nave is the big space in the middle of a traditional **church** building where people gather for **worship**. Nowadays it is often filled with chairs or **pews**. The word 'nave' comes from the word that means 'ship' in Latin.

It's a good image: The people who come to worship are people on the move, travelling together. For a while, the ship is their home. They have not all chosen one another, but are companions for the journey. And **God** is the mariner in charge – looking after the ship, setting the course, steering it through choppy waters and making sure it reaches its destination.

pew

A pew is wooden bench. It is also a challenge. A **church** that was built 500 years ago or more would not have had any seating. People stood up when they came for **worship** (as they do today in some countries). Sometimes there was a bench at one side for those who could not stand. Later on, seating was put into the **nave** for everyone, and the design of seat developed. Some pews had high backs to keep out draughts. Some were even built into compartments with doors at the end. Some people paid rent to the church for their own pew, where they sat every week.

The challenge for churches with pews is that they are not flexible. If you want to use the space in church differently, you can't. It is easy to forget that they are not an essential part of Christianity. They were a practical solution at a particular time. Some churches are finding that different times require different solutions.

pulpit

A pulpit is a stage, although it might not look like one. In a **church** the pulpit is often up a few steps and is a bit like a mini-balcony enclosed with wood or stone. The idea is that the **preacher** in the pulpit can be seen and heard by everyone – just like actors on a stage.

In England, having a **sermon** as part of the service became much more important after the **Reformation**. The oldest pulpits mostly date from then. Some became quite elaborate, with two or three levels. In a three-decker, the bottom level was for a clerk. Otherwise the lower bit had a reading desk in it, and the preacher used the top level.

Where the pulpit was placed depended on the tradition of the church. It might be found at the front and slightly to the side, leaving room for people to get to the **altar** or **communion table**. In some Nonconformist churches, the pulpit will be in the middle to emphasize the importance of the sermon, and the whole service might be led from there.

(see **denomination**)

Name trail: pulpitum *in Latin is the word for a platform, stage or scaffold.*

sanctuary

Church buildings are a bit like pictures of us and **God** and how we get together. The sanctuary is the part of the **chancel** where the **altar** is. The name comes from the Latin word *sanctus*, which means **holy**. This is a holy place because it is where the **bread** and **wine** are placed – where the focus is on God's **love** for us, given in **Jesus**.

'Sanctuary' can also mean safety. A place that is a sanctuary is a safe place, a refuge where nothing bad can get at you.

shrine

Somewhere special for someone special. Originally a shrine meant a box or chest. If you had relics for a **saint** – a lock of hair or a finger bone perhaps – you could keep them here. Sometimes a person's tomb became a shrine. It might have a canopy over it or rails round it, so that it looked like a little building within the **church**. It then became a place of **prayer** in its own right.

vestry

A small room in a **church** building where important things are kept – service registers, records, the safe, and so on. It is also the place for putting on robes or **vestments** for a service. 'Vestry' means 'a place for getting dressed'.

5

people

There are a lot of different people who do things in **church**. There are also different names for the same people, which can be very confusing. This section says something about who's who. (It is in alphabetical order – *not* order of importance!)

archbishop

Put a lot of **dioceses** together and you have a **province**. One of the **bishops** will be in charge of the whole thing, and that is the archbishop.

(see **church organization**)

archdeacon

A **diocese** is divided into groups of **parishes** called deaneries. A few deaneries grouped together make an archdeaconry. The **priest** who looks after the **clergy** and churches in this area is called the archdeacon.

(see **church organization**)

area dean

Local **parish** churches are grouped together into a larger group called a **deanery**. One of the parish **priests** will be the area dean. It is the area dean's job to make sure **clergy** get together for support, training and working together as appropriate. This person will also help parishes in particular need – organizing services when their **vicar** has just moved, for example.

(see **church organization**)

bishop

A **priest** who looks after a large group of churches. A bishop keeps an eye on all the churches in a **diocese,** and works with the **clergy** to help keep Christian **faith** alive in their area. They also speak out at a national level, giving a Christian view about something, offering advice or pointing out how people are affected by government policies.

Name trail: we get our word 'bishop' from the Greek word episkopos – *the* epi *bit means 'upon or over' and the* skopos *bit means 'looking'. A bishop is an 'overseer' who 'looks over' the whole diocese. This became 'bishop' in Old English.*

canon

Clergy who live and work at a **cathedral** are called canons. The word 'canon' means 'rule'. A canon is someone who lives according to a particular rule – in this case, the rules of the **Church.**

chaplain

Someone who is a **minister** in a place that is not a **church.** The name 'chaplain' means someone who takes services in a **chapel.** This might be in a school, hospital, military base or prison, for example. But the **ministry** is not just about taking services somewhere. It is about being a Christian presence. Nowadays many shopping centres or airports have chaplains for example, although they may not have chapels.

choir

A group of singers who help to lead a service.

Sometimes they wear robes, sometimes not. Sometimes they look very formal and walk in long **processions.** Sometimes the choir are all boys and men, sometimes a mixture of everyone. Sometimes they sing on their own, sometimes with everyone else. Sometimes they sing **music** written hundreds of years ago, sometimes what was written last month. What really matters is that the choir's singing helps us all to **worship**.

As Paul says, 'with gratitude in your hearts sing psalms, **hymn**s, and spiritual songs to God' (*Colossians 3.16*).

Church

People gathered together to **worship God**.

It doesn't matter who you are, or whether you gather with others in an ancient cathedral or under a tree at the edge of a desert. When Paul writes to Christians in Corinthian he talks about building up the Church – and he means people, not buildings. He calls these people the *ekklesia*, which means summoned or called out. The Church is the people who are summoned by God to stand up for their **faith** in the **resurrection** of Jesus and the life this brings.

Three further points:

1 The Church is not full of people who think they're perfect, or that they've 'made it', or are better than other people. The opposite is true. Being part of the Church is simply about knowing that you are a unique person, special to God even with all your less-than-great bits, and you want to let God be part of your life.
2 The Church exists all over the world, in lots of different cultures.
3 The Church isn't just made up of people who are alive now. It is about the whole family of God over the centuries – 'angels, archangels, and the whole company of **heaven**'. We don't get the whole picture now, but we are part of something bigger.

(see also section 4, 'buildings & furniture')

Name trail: the Greek word ekklesia, *meaning summoned or called out, gives us 'ecclesiastical', which is used for things to do with the church.*

churchwarden

Clergy come and go, but the **church** in a **parish** remains. Church-wardens are described as 'officers of the **bishop**', and are the people who represent the lay members of the church in the parish. They are elected by people on the **electoral roll**, but are admitted to their role by the bishop. They work in co-operation with the **incumbent**.

Churchwardens are officially responsible for all the things in the church that are not fixed – **chalices** and **patens**, **crosses**, **candle** stands, and so on. They have to keep a list of them, which is called an inventory. More than that, though, they have to be good examples of 'the practices of true **religion**', and 'promote unity and peace' among parishioners. A task for someone with a humble heart, if ever there was one.

clergy

The people who are the ordained ministers in a **church**. The ones who have been trained then ordained to work as a **minister**. You can often spot them by the way they dress – clerical shirts and '**dog collars**' are a kind of uniform.

Clergy are still human beings. Being ordained doesn't make them better than anyone else. But being ordained automatically makes them 'public Christians'. Their jobs will vary, but they all have a role in the community that is about living out in the public eye what it means to be a Christian.

congregation

The people who have come together in a particular place to **worship God**.

Name trail: from the Latin word congregare, *which means 'to collect' or 'gather'.*

curate

Nowadays, 'curate' usually means an assistant **priest** in a **parish** – not the boss, but a helper. Curates often come to a parish when they are first ordained and are still in training.

Strictly speaking, a curate is someone who has the 'cure of **souls**' in a place. 'Cure' means care: the curate has the spiritual care of people. This is still true for all **clergy** no matter how long you have been ordained.

deacon

'Deacon' means 'servant' in Greek. When the **Church** began to grow, the **apostles** found that they couldn't do everything that was needed. People were being neglected, so deacons were appointed to help out (see *Acts 6.1–6*).

In the Church of England, you are ordained as a deacon at the end of your training. You may be ordained **priest** a year later, but whatever job you end up doing, you are always a deacon. Even **bishops** are still deacons, and it is a good reminder that those ordained are always servants of the Church.

dean

The **priest** who is in overall charge of a **cathedral**.

incumbent

Just the name for the person who holds a particular job. In a **parish church**, the incumbent is the **vicar** or **rector**.

laity, lay person

The laity are the people who are not the **clergy**. A **church** is usually made up of a larger number of lay people and a smaller number of clergy – often just one **priest**.

Every single person is important in the life of the church. While it is the priest's job to preside at communion, lay people usually take part in services in lots of ways – for example, as **servers**, leading **music**, reading, leading **prayers**, taking up the offering, serving the **bread** and **wine**. Many people have leadership roles outside services too, as home group leaders, youth group leaders, or as **PCC** members who make decisions with the **vicar** about the life of the church. For other people, 'being church' will be focused in the home, school or workplace. This is just as important as anything else mentioned here.

The words 'laity' and 'lay' are used more generally than just in church. A lay person is someone who is not a professional. They might have a general understanding of a topic, but would not be expected to know the detail.

Name trail: from laos *in Greek, meaning 'people'.*

minister, ministry

In Christian denominations that don't have **priests**, the person appointed to be in charge is often called the minister. In the Anglican Church, a minister can be **clergy** or **lay**. 'Ministry' describes the work they do.

*Name trail: 'minister' is a Latin word meaning servant. When the **Bible** was translated from Greek into Latin, 'minister' was the word used for the Greek word* diakonos *(deacon).*

pastor

Another word for the **minister** of a church. A **congregation** might have more than one pastor, or it might be the name used for the person in charge of the congregation.

Using this word gives a particular emphasis: in Latin, 'pastor' means shepherd. The pastors are the ones who look after the flocks of sheep. In John's Gospel, **Jesus** says, 'I am the good shepherd. The good shepherd lays down his life for the sheep' (*John 10.11*). Calling someone a pastor suggests that their job is about looking after people – not just their practical needs but spiritual care too.

preacher

The person who gives the **sermon**. In a service, one or more passages from the **Bible** will be read. The preacher's job is to explain this to the **congregation** and make links with life now. A preacher might not be an ordained **minister**, but a preacher does need to know what he or she is talking about. Preachers will usually have spent some time studying the Bible and thinking through ideas about **God**.

priest

Go back a long way, into the time of the Old Testament, and you find that the priests were the people who worked in the Temple. People brought things to **sacrifice** to **God**, and the priests took them and made the offering. (You can read the detail in the book of Leviticus.) So you could say that, like now, a priest was a servant of God and a servant of the people.

Using the name 'priest' for the leader of the Christian **congregation** carried on from this because the idea of a priest and the link with sacrifice is important.

- **Jesus** made a sacrifice – he gave his life for us.
- He knew this would happen when he shared **bread** and **wine** with his **friends** at the Last Supper.
- When we come to communion we share in what he did.
- The idea of offering is important: he gave his life for us; we offer ourselves to God.
- This is at the heart of the **Church**'s existence.
- In the book of Hebrews the writer uses the imagery of the Temple and its **worship** to talk about Jesus and Christian worship.

- We are all to be like the priests and the Temple. Peter urges people: 'like living stones, let yourselves be built into a spiritual house, to be a **holy** priesthood, to offer spiritual sacrifices . . .', and says, 'But you are a chosen race, a royal priesthood, a holy nation, God's own people . . .' (*1 Peter 2.5, 9*).

So we call our spiritual leaders priests. They help us focus on God.

Reader

Not just the person who is reading in a service! A Reader is a **lay person** who has been trained and licensed to help in the **ministry** of the local Anglican **church**. Reader ministry is usually focused on preaching and teaching, but may include other things. When robed, Readers can be spotted by the fact that they wear a blue **scarf**.

rector

Yet another name for the **priest** who is in charge of a **parish church**. Nowadays there's very little difference at all between a **vicar** and a rector.

It used to be different. A few hundred years ago or more the Church owned a lot of land. Whoever was in charge of a church was allowed to keep the **tithe**s. This meant that the rector had the right to one-tenth of all that the land produced – crops, milk from its cows, eggs, etc. The rector wasn't always the priest who lived and worked at the local church, though. He might have been abbot of the local monastery, or in charge of a larger church not far away. In this case there would probably have been a vicar doing the job for him – only the vicar didn't get the tithes.
(see **vicar**)

rural dean

Like an **area dean**, the rural dean is one of the local **vicars** who looks after all the clergy in the **deanery**. (A long time ago they were all called rural deans, but that doesn't make much sense in a city.)

(see **area dean**)

server

Well, remembering that we are talking about people not computers, it is as it says really – a server is someone who serves others. During a **church** service, servers might do a variety of things: carry the **cross** in a **procession**, help set the table for communion, receive the collection, receive the **bread** and **wine** if they are brought up from the **congregation**, or ring bells at particular points in the service. They help to make the service happen, and the service is about enabling people to hear and receive **God**. Servers are not essential, but they are important.

sidesman/sideswoman/sidesperson

These are the very important people who will usually be found near the entrance to the **church** before a service – welcoming people and handing out service books. Anyone on the **electoral roll** is eligible to be a sidesperson.

There is a bit more to it than that, though. Officially the sidespeople are assistants to the **churchwardens**. That means that they too are supposed to 'promote the cause of true **religion** in the **parish**', and 'maintain order and decency' – especially at the time of a service. So on the off chance that there's a brawl over the **hymn** books, you know who to call on.

verger/virger

When you are leading a service in **church**, there are all sorts of practical things to think of.

- Where is the collection plate?
- Are the **chalice** and **paten** ready for communion?
- Are there chairs out for the bride and groom at the **wedding**?
- Where are the **marriage** registers?
- What **vestments** are needed today?
- Have we got a **paschal candle**?
- Is there any water in the **font**?
- Has anyone replaced that light bulb at the **lectern**?
- And many more . . .

In some churches, all these things will be done by the verger. Not all churches have a verger; it depends a bit on the tradition. A **cathedral** might have a team of vergers. A small **parish** church might have someone who is very part time. What they do varies from place to place. Apart from doing all the practical things mentioned above, they might also take part in services, carrying their 'verge' – basically a long wooden stick – to lead a **procession**. They are very important people – the sort you miss if you move to a church where there isn't a verger!

vicar

A very common name for the person who is in charge of a **parish church**. Nowadays, quite a lot of vicars are part of a team. They may be in charge of one church but belong to a team **ministry** of several churches together, led by the team **rector**. But, did you know:

- 'vicar' comes from the Latin word *vicarius*, which means 'substitute'? A vicar was someone who looked after a parish on behalf of someone else. If the church had been set up by a monastery, the vicar looked after it on behalf of the religious community at the monastery (who had the right to the **tithes**).

- the word is also used to refer to someone who is the substitute or representative of **God** on earth? Not a bad reminder for all **clergy** really, as they are seen as the public face of the Church.
- in the Roman Catholic Church, the Pope is sometimes called the Vicar of **Christ**?

6

stuff to do with services

absolution

After we have said a prayer of **confession** in a **church** service, the **priest** stands up and declares that we are forgiven. This is the absolution. It means saying that **God** forgives us, we are pardoned, free of the burden or things we know we've done wrong. We can make a fresh start.

Of course we can admit our wrongs to God and receive his forgiveness when we are on our own. Sometimes, though, it helps to hear someone else say it to us. It is part of the role of the **priest** because in Matthew's Gospel, when **Jesus** is teaching his **disciples** about forgiveness, he says, 'whatever you bind on earth will be bound in **heaven**, and whatever you loose on earth will be loosed in heaven' (*Matthew 18.18*).

acolyte

Someone who is an assistant to the **priest** during a service. Acolytes often carry the **candles** in a **procession**, and may help with setting the **altar** or table for communion. They are often part of a team of **servers**.

alb see **vestments**

bread

- Granary. White. Wholemeal. Pitta bread. Black bread. Rye bread. Chapatti. Loaf. Roll. French stick. Baguette. A basic food, just about everywhere.

- When **Jesus** shared bread before he died, he said, 'This is my **body**, broken for you.' That bread took on a whole new meaning.
- We are part of that meaning. As **friends** of Jesus, we share bread. Like the first **disciples**, we are drawn into the events of that last supper. We share his **suffering** and we live out his new life.

cassock see **vestments**

chalice

A drinking cup with a stem like a **wine** glass. It's often made of silver, but can also be pottery. At **Holy Communion** wine is poured into it during the Eucharistic Prayer – enough for everyone present to have a sip from the one cup when the **bread** and wine are shared.

Name trail: from the Latin word calix, *meaning cup.*

chasuble see **vestments**

choruses

Songs that are sung as part of an act of **worship**. If it is called a chorus, it is usually short and may be repeated more than once.

confession

When you've got something inside you that's a secret, hidden from everyone else, you sometimes need to get it out – but in a safe way. This is what confession is about. There are nearly always things we've said or done or failed to do, or wished we'd done differently. These things sit inside us, and even if we push them out of sight they are still there. When we say a **prayer** of confession, we are bringing these things out – saying to **God**, 'I know this is wrong and I don't want it to be part of me any more'. It's a bit like when old lunch wrappers or apple cores fall to the bottom of your bag. They might be out of sight, but after a while they cause a stink and need to come out.

In a **church** service we confess together. It's a really important part of Christianity that we don't just ask God to forgive us individually. We are all part of a community, all part of the human race – and human beings can do horrible things to each other. We make a mess of the world God has given us to look after. Corporate confession is about the bigger picture. We know we make mistakes here too, and so ask for God's forgiveness and help to have a go at making it better.

(see **sin**)

Name trail: 'corporate' comes from the Latin word corpus, *which means* '**body**'. *Corporate confession is about the whole* **Body of Christ** *admitting wrongdoing to God, not just as individuals.*

cope see **vestments**

Creed

When Christians come together to **worship** in **church**, the service will often include a statement that summarizes what we believe. This is called the Creed. There are two main creeds that are used: the Apostles' Creed (at morning and evening prayer) and the Nicene Creed (at communion services). They are both very ancient. Working out the right words was an important part of the Church working out exactly what it did and did not believe.

Name trail: 'creed' simply comes from credo – *the first word of the Creed in Latin, which means 'I believe'.*

Eucharist see **Holy Communion**

Holy Communion

There are four names commonly used for the service where Christians share **bread** and **wine** together in the name of **Jesus**: the Eucharist, Holy Communion, the Lord's Supper and the Mass.

Each name emphasizes a different aspect of what the service is about.

- **Eucharist.** The word means thanksgiving. In the service that's what we do – thank **God** for what he has given us and done for us.
- **Holy Communion.** Being together with **God**. Communion is about sharing, doing something together, being in a relationship – not just me and God, but me and you and God. Together we receive the love that flows from God's selfless action in Jesus.
- **Lord's Supper.** The Lord is Jesus, and the supper reminds us of the last supper, just before he was arrested. He shared bread and wine with his **friends** and taught them something more about what was to happen. Sitting and eating together is special. We are Jesus' friends. We learn from him. We have supper with him too.
- **Mass.** Most commonly used in the Roman Catholic Church, the name 'mass' comes from the Latin words that were used right at the end of the service: *Ite, missa est*. It's a bit difficult to translate, but in English this usually comes out as 'Go, the Mass is ended.' That doesn't just mean that it's time for coffee and biscuits. It means, 'Turn outwards. Take what you have received and share it with the world.'

(see also **sacrament**)

hymn

A hymn is a song to or about **God**.

There are three things involved in a good hymn: the words, the **music**, and you and me.

- The words have got to be something worth saying. Good words express Christian beliefs, often better than we can ourselves. Good words challenge us about our beliefs.

- The music has to match the words and help them come alive. It's no good having a song about how wonderful God is if it is set to a musical dirge. It's no good having a jolly tune for words that express our sadness to God.
- It's not much good having either of these if there's nobody to bring them alive. Joining in with hymns in **worship** is about putting ourselves on the line and saying 'I believe this too'.

incense

Grains of resin or gum, which release a scented smoke when placed on burning charcoal. Incense is most often used in the more 'high' or '**Catholic**' churches.

It has an important symbolism. In Roman times it was used to signify various things, including being used as a mark of honour and adoration. However, in the Christian **Church** today its main significance is also its most ancient – a symbol of the **prayers** of the people rising to **God**.

> I call upon you, O LORD; come quickly to me;
>   give ear to my voice when I call to you.
> Let my prayer be counted as incense before you,
>   and the lifting up of my hands as an evening sacrifice.
>
> *(Psalm 141.1–2)*

liturgy

'The liturgy' refers to the form of public **worship**, the service as a whole – the order of words and **music** used.

Name trail: 'liturgy' comes from leitourgia *in Greek, which means 'service', 'worship', 'offering' and 'ministry'. It reminds us that coming to worship is not so much about what we get out of it, but about giving something of ourselves.*

Lord's Supper see **Holy Communion**

Mass see **Holy Communion**

mitre see **vestments**

music

Organ. Piano. Trumpet. Guitar. Flute. Drum. Tambourine. Band. Choir. **Worship** group. Music group. CD player. **Hymn**-singing. Psalm-chanting. Solos. Unaccompanied singing. However it is done, it's nearly always there.

Music is a major part of worship. It's a natural way of respond- ing to **God**. It is very diverse. You might be a music-maker. You may prefer to listen.

Music is a major part of **church**, but is not the most important thing. If it's put above all else it is seriously out of tune. Music is a servant that enables the whole **congregation** to worship God. If it lifts the heart it is good. If it gets in the way then something's wrong.

paten

The plate or shallow dish that holds the **bread** for communion.

prayers

A lot of praying happens in **church**. We often say the same prayers at each service, and the words are printed in the service book. We can say them without thinking. Do we really mean what we are saying? Well, there are two points about this.

1 It can be hard to mean it every time, but it is the job of who- ever is leading the service to help make this happen. A few introductory words and a bit of silence to give people time to think before speaking is very helpful.
2 The great thing about set words that people have been saying for centuries is that it reminds us that we are part of something

bigger. There may be important things to say, even if we don't feel like it (and sometimes we might even feel better after we've done it).

'The prayers' during a service can often refer to the prayers of intercession. To intercede means to be a go-between. Intercession means to ask for something on behalf of someone else. In the prayers of intercession, we bring before **God** the needs of the world we live in.

procession

One of the ways you know that the service is starting is that whoever is leading comes to the front. It might just be the **vicar,** or perhaps a **choir** too, and maybe **servers** with the **cross, candles** and a **Bible.** The more people you have, the more important it is for them to walk to their places in an orderly way. That makes a procession. *But* – a procession isn't just about moving around the building. It's also a way of saying 'Something's happening – the action is moving on – look!' Processions are to do with the drama that we are part of. Here are some other examples.

- Your church might have a Gospel procession – someone carries the Bible, another comes to read it, and two **acolytes** might lead the way carrying candles. Instead of someone coming to read the Gospel from the front, the Bible is carried down the **nave** into the midst of the people and read from there. It dramatizes the **incarnation: God** being among his people.
- There might be an offertory procession. **Clergy** move to the **altar,** and the **bread** and **wine** for communion are brought up by people in the **congregation.** The focus has changed again, from hearing God's word to sharing the **sacrament** of **Holy Communion.**

scarf see **vestments**

sermon

A sermon is like a meal: it can be tasty stuff full of good ingredients that will feed our **faith**, or it can be chock full of indigestible junk food that just makes us unhealthy.

To preach a sermon is to answer questions and make connections. What did that **Bible** reading mean? What does it tell us about **God**? How does that affect me now? Where is God in what is going on?

A good sermon should also raise at least one question: what am I going to do about it?

stole see **vestments**

surplice see **vestments**

vestments

'Vestment' is just a word for a piece of clothing. Vestments help us to see the people wearing them as **ministers** of the **Church**. The clothes are self-effacing: 'For this time when I am doing this job what I wear covers my individuality so that the focus can be on what I'm doing, and why I'm doing it.'

- It's like wearing a uniform – we can recognize the job firefighters or police officers do by the clothes they wear.
- It's about being set apart to do a particular job in a particular setting – I may be a district nurse all the time, but I only wear my uniform when I am on the job.
- It's about being part of something bigger than 'just me' – what is going on in church is about all of us gathered together, worshipping with 'the angels, and archangels and all the company of **heaven** . . .'

Of course, it is a bit odd that most of the vestments commonly worn by people during church services have their roots in the Roman Empire, not the twenty-first century. At bottom, they are basically indoor tunics or outdoor cloaks. There are lots of different kinds of vestment, but the most common ones are:

- **alb:** a long white or ivory-coloured tunic, often worn with a girdle (a cord) tied at the waist. It is usually worn by the **priest**s leading a service of **Holy Communion**.

  *At the time of the early Church, this sort of thing was usually worn by professional people. It had become a specifically Christian form of dress by the early 400s. Of all the different kinds of vestments, this is the one that ties in with a specific biblical image. Look at Revelation 7.9 and you'll find that all those people joining in with the **worship** of heaven are wearing white robes.*

  Name trail: 'alb' is simply a shortened form of the Latin word albus, *meaning 'white'.*

- **cassock:** also a full-length tunic with long sleeves, but it comes in lots of different colours for lots of different people. **Clergy** usually wear black cassocks, so do **Readers**, but they can also be found in a variety of reds, greens, blues and beiges, worn by **verger**s, **server**s and **choir** members. It's a basic garment, often worn underneath a surplice.

  This was what Romans normally wore, but by about the 500s the fashion changed to a shorter tunic. Clergy kept the ankle-length coat, usually in plain black, as a way of marking themselves out from the crowd.

- **chasuble:** this looks like a kind of poncho and is worn by the priest who is 'celebrant' or 'president' at Holy Communion (the person leading the service). It is usually the right **colour** for the season and can be decorated with elaborate embroidery.

The chasuble comes from the Roman outdoor cloak worn by women and men of all classes. It seems to have been used for clergy in this way since about the 700s.

- **cope:** a cloak. Like the chasuble it can be highly decorated and is usually only worn for special occasions in larger churches and **cathedrals**.

  Originally, this kind of Roman cloak would have had a hood. If you see a cope with an odd triangular flap at the back of the neck, this is a 'left-over hood'.

- **mitre:** a hat that has been part of a **bishop**'s robes for at least the past thousand years. From the front it looks shaped like an arch. A mitre is worn during some church ceremonies and is a mark of the bishop's authority.
- **scarf:** this is not a scarf worn for warmth or decoration! It is properly called a preaching scarf, and is a sign of the **authority** to preach. Ordained **clergy** wear a black scarf, and Readers a blue one. It is a non-eucharistic garment, meaning it is worn at services of morning or evening prayer and not normally at communion services.
- **stole:** a long coloured strip of cloth worn over an alb by ordained ministers. The stole is received by **deacons** at their ordination, worn over the left shoulder and tied or fastened diagonally under the right arm. When a deacon is ordained priest, the stole is unfastened and hangs down equally on both sides. It is worn at services of Holy Communion and matches the liturgical colours of the season.

  In Greek, stola *just means robe. The church use comes from the scarf that Roman senators wore as a mark of their rank.*

- **surplice:** the white garment worn over a cassock. It has a wide neck where the fabric is gathered, wide three-quarter-length sleeves, and is usually about knee length. Clergy might wear one at a non-eucharistic service. Where robed choirs wear cassocks they nearly always wear a surplice over the top for services.

wine

About 25 years after **Jesus' death** and **resurrection**, Paul repeated the words Jesus had spoken at that last supper before he was arrested. When he took the cup of wine he said, 'This cup is the new covenant in my blood.' From that moment, the wine meant something new for Jesus' **friends**. As a symbol of his blood, the wine gets to the heart of what Christian **faith** is about: in Jesus' dying and rising, there's a new start with **God**.

Jesus also said, '*Do* this . . . in remembrance of me.' Join in. Live out that new start.

worship

Worship goes on all the time; we just join in. One of the **prayers** in the communion service talks about us worshipping with the 'angels and archangels and all the company of **heaven**'. When we worship we are surrendering ourselves to one who is bigger and more important than we are. But one thing is essential: love. We worship knowing we are loved by **God**, and with love give ourselves back to him.

Name trail: our word 'worship' comes from the Old English word weorthscype. *It's the same root that gives us the word 'worth'. To worship someone is to recognize their value.*

7

events & seasons

The Christian year starts with Advent Sunday, so the first part of this section goes through the year in chronological order. Churches often use colour to mark out the different seasons and festivals (see the explanation on p. 77).

Advent

It's the word used to describe the period of about four weeks leading up to **Christmas**, and the name means 'coming'. The idea: as we prepare to celebrate **God**'s first coming to us in **Jesus**, we also think about the promise that he will come again in the **second coming**. What do we mean when we say '**Christ** will come again'? What difference does it make to us?
Liturgical colour: purple.

Christmas

Christ-mas: the celebration of **Christ**. We celebrate **Jesus**' birth. We give gifts because **God** has given himself in Jesus. We receive gifts because in Jesus God has put himself among us. Take 'Christ' out of 'Christmas' and it loses its meaning.
Liturgical colour: gold or white.

Epiphany

This is the time following the **Christmas** season when we think particularly about how **God** shows himself to us in **Jesus**. It starts with celebrating the visit of the Wise Men (or Magi) to Jesus. Their gifts – weird presents for a baby – say something about who he is:

- gold – for a **king**
- frankincense – used in **worship**, this says that Jesus is something to do with the worship of God
- myrrh – as one of the spices used to prepare a **body** for burial, this hints at **suffering** to come.

The Epiphany season varies in length, depending on when **Easter** comes. The focus is on how God is made known as Jesus begins his **ministry**.
Liturgical colour: gold or white.

Name trail: from the Greek epiphaino, *meaning 'to appear', 'reveal' or 'display'.*

Presentation (also called **Candlemas**)

Like other Jewish baby boys at the time, when he was 40 days old **Jesus** was presented in the Temple in Jerusalem by his parents. There they offered a **sacrifice**, as it said in the Jewish law (see *Leviticus 12.1–8*). This is remembered at the feast of the Presentation. It marks a turning point, and the end of the **Epiphany** season. We are still focused on the baby Jesus, but Simeon's words to Mary in the Temple point towards the **suffering** that is to come: 'This child is destined for the falling and the rising of many in Israel . . . and a sword will pierce your own **soul** too' (*Luke 2.34–35*). Following the Presentation, we begin counting Sundays before Lent.
Liturgical colour: gold or white.

*Name trail: this is also known as Candlemas because in some churches a **procession** of **candles** was part of the event. Simeon describes this baby as 'a light for revelation to the Gentiles' (Luke 2.32), and we still use candles in the service to remind us of this.*

Shrove Tuesday

The day before Ash Wednesday. 'Shrove' comes from the old English word 'shrive', which we don't use any more. It was all about someone hearing your **confession**, giving you a **penance**, and then – hopefully – the all-clear: a pardon for anything you've confessed to doing wrong. It was part of preparing for **Lent**.

Traditionally, people would clear their houses of any foods that could not be part of the Lenten fast. They would cook them up together in a pan, making pan-cakes. Shrove Tuesday is also known as Pancake Day, when of course, pancakes are eaten.

Liturgical colour: green.

Ash Wednesday

The first day of **Lent**, and so the beginning of a time of **penitence**. Ash Wednesday is a day for being realistic about what it is to be a human being. **God** made us good, but his image in us gets spoiled. An Ash Wednesday service reminds us of this.

Traditionally the palm crosses from the previous year are burned to ash and mixed with oil to make a paste. During the service, the **minister**s dip their thumb in the paste and draw a **cross** on the foreheads of the people, saying, 'Remember that you are dust, and to dust you shall return . . .'

Liturgical colour: purple.

As in Genesis 2.7: 'then the LORD *God formed man from the dust of the ground, and breathed into his nostrils the breath of life; and the man became a living being'.*

Lent

This is the name for the period of six weeks and four days between **Ash Wednesday** and Easter Day. It has always been a time of **penitence** when we prepare ourselves for the great celebration of the **resurrection** at **Easter**. Traditionally people got rid of the luxuries in life – no meat, for example, and fish on Fridays. The **discipline** of **fasting** was often part of observing Lent,

71

mirroring the 40 days Jesus spent in the desert immediately after his **baptism**.

Of course, six weeks and four days makes 46 days not 40, but as Sunday is always the day of resurrection, the Sundays are not counted.

Liturgical colour: purple.

Passiontide

The couple of weeks at the end of **Lent** when the focus is on the Passion, or **suffering,** of **Jesus**.

Liturgical colour: purple in the first of these weeks and then red in Holy Week (white for Maundy Thursday).

Name trail: we get this word from passio *in Latin, which comes from the verb meaning 'suffer'.*

Palm Sunday

This is the Sunday that marks the beginning of **Holy Week.** We remember how **Jesus** rode into Jerusalem on a donkey, when people waved palm branches and acclaimed him as **King. Crosses** made out of palm leaves are often given out on this Sunday and blessed as part of the service. They remind us that by the end of the week, the one who was welcomed was crucified.

Liturgical colour: red.

Holy Week

The week of **Palm Sunday** to Holy Saturday. The week takes us through the events that followed Jesus' entry into Jerusalem, leading up to his **crucifixion** on **Good Friday,** and the grief and silence that follow. Holy Week gives way to the joy that comes on **Easter** Day.

Liturgical colour: red (white on Maundy Thursday).

Maundy Thursday

The day before Good Friday when the Church remembers the events of the Last Supper. Churches often include foot-washing on this day to remind us that at this supper Jesus washed his disciples' feet (see John 13.1–11).

Liturgical colour: white.

Name trail: in Latin translations of the Bible, when Jesus talks about what he has done in washing the disciples' feet, he says he has given them a mandatum novum, *which means a new commandment (John 13.34). 'Maundy' comes from this word* mandatum.

Good Friday

The day in **Holy Week** when **Jesus** was crucified. It seems odd to call it 'good' when we remember such a dreadful event. However, if Jesus had not been crucified, there would have been no **resurrection**. This day shows us just how much **God** loves us.

Liturgical colour: red.

Easter

The celebration of **Jesus' resurrection**. Beginning on Easter Sunday, it lasts for 50 days up to **Pentecost**.

At Easter people often give chocolate Easter eggs, as the egg is a sign of new life and reminds us of the new life **God** gives us in Jesus.

Liturgical colour: gold or white on Easter Day, and then white until Pentecost.

Ascension Day

This comes 40 days after **Easter** Day and is when we remember **Jesus** being taken up, or ascending, into **heaven**. It is described in Acts 1.6–11. It is as if the time when he was with his **disciples** after the **resurrection** was a gift, but it had to end so that the gift of the **Holy Spirit** could be given.

'Ascensiontide' is sometimes used to describe the ten days between Ascension Day and **Pentecost**.
Liturgical colour: gold or white.

Pentecost (also known as **Whitsun**)

Sometimes called 'the birthday of the **Church**', Pentecost is the day when we celebrate the gift of the **Holy Spirit** to the **disciples**. It comes ten days after **Ascension**, and 50 days after **Easter**. In the book of Acts, Luke describes events that transformed Jesus' disciples. They experienced the sound of rushing wind, the appearance of tongues like flames over each one of them, and the ability to speak in different languages. This powerful experience of **God**'s Spirit enabled them to become the strong and visionary leaders who continued his **ministry** and built up the emerging church (*Acts 2.1–4*).

This happened at Pentecost, a Jewish harvest festival that took place 50 days after Passover. The name means '50'.

Whitsun or Whit Sunday is the name traditionally used for Pentecost. The 'Whit' bit means 'white'. It was called this because at Pentecost people who were newly baptized would wear white clothing to represent their new life in **Christ**.
Liturgical colour: red.

Trinity Sunday

The Sunday after **Pentecost** is Trinity Sunday, and it is there for a very good reason.

The weeks around **Easter** are very dramatic: the tension and despair of **Holy Week**; death and grief followed by the joy of **resurrection**; the departure of **Jesus** at the **Ascension**, and the extraordinary gift of the **Holy Spirit** at Pentecost. Following Jesus through all of this must have been like being on an emotional roller-coaster.

Trinity Sunday is a day for taking a step back and celebrating the **God** who is at the heart of these events: we celebrate the gift

of God in being among us; the wholeness of God as Father, Son and Holy Spirit; and we rejoice at our part in his life.
Liturgical colour: gold or white.
(see **Trinity**)

Transfiguration

Jesus takes three close **friends** for a walk up a mountain. So far, nothing unusual. Then quite out of the blue:

- Jesus looked different – dazzlingly bright;
- Moses was there with Elijah, both talking to Jesus;
- Peter didn't know what to say, but said it anyway – asking if they should make three '**shrines**';
- they heard a heavenly voice calling Jesus 'beloved Son', and saying they should listen to him.

Then it was back to normal.

Put yourself in their place: would your friends believe you if you told them what happened? Fortunately it was okay, because at that point Jesus told them not to tell anyone – yet. Later they did, and you can read about it in the Gospels (*Mark 9.2–13*; *Matthew 17.1–13*; *Luke 9.28–36*).

The Transfiguration is important because:

1 two of the most revered prophets from the Jewish tradition are seen affirming Jesus' **ministry**;
2 it was very important to have two witnesses to back up the truth of an event;
3 they speak of Jesus' **death** and **resurrection**, which his **disciple**s don't yet understand;
4 **God's** glory is shown in Jesus;
5 Jesus is affirmed by God as his Son.

The Transfiguration is remembered by the Church on 6 August.
Liturgical colour: gold or white.

Name trail: 'transfiguration' comes from the Latin word transfigurare, *which means 'to change the shape or appearance'.*

THE CHRISTIAN FESTIVAL
DECIDING WHETHER WE WILL BE GOING OR NOT

* * *

baptism

Baptism is about new beginnings and being loved by **God**. Three symbols in a baptism service remind us what it is about:

1 *Water*: we are washed clean. It's not mud and dirt that has to go, but the deeper things that make us unclean inside – harsh words, bad thoughts, unkindness, etc. (see **sin**)

2 *The cross*: we are marked with the sign of the cross. This reminds us that God has shown his love for us in what he did through **Jesus' death** and **resurrection**.

3 *A lighted candle*: a reminder that as God's forgiven and cleansed people we are carrying the light of jesus so that it shines out in our everyday lives.

Christening

Another word for **baptism**. It means what it says: 'Christ-ening' – 'to make like **Christ**'.

colours

Using different colours in **church** is a way of helping us live out the Christian story through the year. They are often called liturgical colours because they are to do with the **liturgy**, the **worship** of the Church. Different seasons are marked by different colours. The significance of the colours and what they remind us of are:

- *green* for life and growth: used for the 'ordinary time' when we are simply focusing on getting on with ordinary life;
- *red* for fire and blood: used when we focus on the **Holy Spirit** at **Pentecost**, and on some **saints**' days, especially those who were **martyrs**;
- *purple* for reflection: used for times of **penitence** when we think about ourselves and our behaviour, such as during **Advent** and **Lent**;
- *white or gold* for celebration: used at **Christmas**, **Easter** and **Ascension**.

The sort of things that change colour are the **altar** cloth, the cloth that hangs from the **lectern** and **pulpit**, and the **stole** and **chasuble** worn by the **priest** and **deacon**.

confirmation

We often think of this as being the service where people become full members of the **Church**, although that's not quite true. If they were baptized as babies their parents and godparents would have made promises on their behalf. At confirmation they make the **baptism** promises themselves. The **bishop** is there, and confirms the baptism that happened when they were younger. The bishop prays for the **Holy Spirit** to be with the person. They are confirmed in the Christian **faith**.

Fascinating fact: Confirmation – a historical accident?

*Bishops used to go to churches to take part in all baptisms. It was a great celebration: people were washed, anointed and prayed over as they entered the Christian faith. But as the Church grew and spread, bishops could not visit every **parish** in their **diocese** very often – it was too big. At the same time, people believed it was very important for babies to be baptized very soon after birth. They thought that if not, the child might not go to **heaven**. So **priests** would normally baptize a baby, but wait for the bishop to come to do the other bits. It might be a long time before this happened, so gradually it became the pattern that people would be baptized as babies, then confirmed when they were older. The basic reason why baptism and confirmation were separated was forgotten.*

funeral

The service that takes place when a person dies. It is important for several reasons:

- we can say thank you for the life of the person who has died;
- we can express our sadness to **God**;
- we remember that all life comes from God and goes on beyond what we experience now;
- we commend the person to God's loving care.

ordination

The service at which people are ordained as **deacons** and **priests**. They make promises to serve, are prayed for by the **bishop**, and receive a **Bible** as a sign of their **authority** to carry out this **ministry** in the **Church**.

requiem

This Latin word means 'rest'. A requiem or requiem **Mass** is a **funeral** service that includes **Holy Communion**. It is common in the Roman Catholic Church and sometimes happens in the more Anglo-Catholic part of the Church of England.

wedding

A wedding celebrates the **marriage** of two people. A wedding service in **church** recognizes that it takes three to make a good marriage – bride, bridegroom and **God**. Unlike a civic ceremony, the marriage service includes listening to God, promises made in the presence of God, **prayers** for the couple, and God's **blessing** on their life together.

8

bits that don't fit anywhere else

Anglican Church see **church organization**

APCM (Annual Parochial Church Meeting)

Every **parish** has a meeting once a year at which **churchwardens**, **sidespersons** and members of the PCC are elected; the church finances are reviewed; reports on the previous year's activities are read, and future plans are set out. This is called the Annual Parochial Church Meeting, or APCM for short.

Apocrypha

The books of the **Bible** accepted by all Christian churches are called the canon. The writings of the Apocrypha are the ones that didn't quite make it into the canon. They are mostly written later than those in the Old Testament but before the time of **Jesus**. Like the Old Testament collection they include story, prophecy, proverbs, history and **prayers**. Some Bibles include the Apocrypha between the Old and New Testaments.

These writings are sometimes called 'deutero-canonical', meaning secondary canon. They are also described as 'inter-testamental' – coming from the time between the Old Testament and the New Testament.

archdeaconry see **church organization**

boring

Dull. If something's boring, it doesn't grab us. We might want to be engaged, caught up in something, feel it's got under our skin, but it's not happening for us. We are bored. Sometimes this happens in **church** (whatever age you are).

We might be right. Something needs to change. It might be one of two things.

1 Church: in which case, don't switch off; get stuck in. Talk to people about why church is the way it is; find out more; say how you feel and why. This might help others to think about church differently. It could lead to opportunities for change.
2 Us: church isn't just about what we get out of it; it's about what we put into it too. What do we bring to God? What do we give to the other people there? What part do I or could I play? How do I fit into the Body of Christ?

catholic

1 'Catholic' means 'universal'. That is what the Christian **Church** is – it's everywhere. That is why in the **Creed** we say that we believe in the 'holy catholic church'. However –
2 'Catholic' is often used to refer to the Roman Catholic Church. This is found in many countries, but is governed by the Pope in Rome.

An Anglo-Catholic church is a church where the traditions and practices associated with the Roman Catholic Church are valued, even if they are not central to the Church of England as a whole.

churchmanship

Churches vary enormously. Talk of 'churchmanship' is a way of describing the character of a **church** or church leader. Just as a person might prefer one band to another, one TV programme, writer, composer or newspaper to another, so people will like one emphasis of Christian practice more than another.

It is a shorthand way of indicating what is most highly valued.

(see **catholic, evangelical, liberal**)

church organization

- **parish**: every church in the Church of England is set in a parish. The whole of the UK is divided into parishes, and this is the area served by the local church. The **vicar** is vicar of the parish, not just of the church. Every parish elects people to be members of the **PCC** – Parochial Church Council. The PCC shares the church leadership with the vicar.
- **deanery**: parishes are grouped together to form deaneries. The deanery is looked after by one of its **clergy**, who is also the **rural dean** or **area dean**. Clergy and **lay people** in the deanery work together, and representatives from each parish meet regularly at a deanery synod.
- **archdeaconry**: several deaneries together belong to an archdeaconry, which is looked after by an **archdeacon**. Archdeacons meet regularly with their rural deans and with their **bishop**s.
- **diocese**: just like the country being divided into counties, the Church of England is divided into dioceses. There are over 40 in total in the Church of England. Every diocese has a diocesan bishop who is in charge of the whole area. The diocesan bishop is assisted by a suffragan or assistant bishop. Decisions within the diocese are made by the diocesan synod. This is made up of bishops, clergy and lay people from each deanery.
- **province**: the Church of England has two provinces: the province of York in the north, and the province of Canterbury in the south. Each is looked after by an **archbishop**, who also still has some responsibility as a diocesan bishop.
- **General Synod**: the Church of England is governed by a kind of 'mini-parliament' called the General Synod. It is made up of

three groups or 'houses': the House of Laity, the House of Clergy, and the House of Bishops. Clergy and lay members are elected within each diocese. All the big issues that affect the church and church practice are discussed in the General Synod. Decisions that need to be made are voted on by all members. For something to go ahead it needs to be passed by a two-thirds majority in each of these three 'houses'.

The Anglican Church extends beyond England itself and consists of 38 provinces across the world. Many of these are Anglican because missionaries travelled to these places from the Church of England. The churches they helped to start are now all part of independent provinces that are in communion with the Church of England – this means that they are part of the same family and are in contact with each other. They have provincial bishops meetings, and once every ten years come together at the Lambeth Conference. The Archbishop of Canterbury is the focus of the Anglican Church worldwide.

conservative

This describes someone who is likely to be cautious about change and wants to preserve the traditions of the **Church**. For example, conservative **Evangelicals** are Christians who have a very strong sense of wanting to live according to the same values that they see in the **Bible**. Conservative **Catholics** are Christians who will not want to change the things upheld by the Roman Catholic Church or challenge the **authority** of the Pope. (For the opposite, see **liberal**.)

denomination

Anglican. Baptist. Congregational. Coptic. Episcopal. Greek Orthodox. Independent Evangelical. Methodist. Pentecostal. Presbyterian. Roman Catholic. Russian Orthodox. United Reformed.

These are all part of the Christian **Church**, just different denominations – branches of the same family tree.

deanery see church organization

diocese see church organization

dog collar

Clergy usually wear a white circular collar at the neck of their clerical shirt. Some shirts are designed so that just a bit of the white collar shows at the front; others are designed so that the white collar shows all the way round. This clerical collar is commonly known as a dog collar – for the very simple reason that it looks like one.

Of course, you can make more of this: a dog's collar is where the lead clips on so that the animal can be directed by its owner. Similarly, the clergy who wear this clerical 'dog collar' submit themselves to being led by **God**.

electoral roll

In effect the electoral roll is a list of adult **church** members. To be on the electoral roll you need to be baptized, over 16 years old and living in the parish. If you are not living in the **parish** but have been worshipping at the church for at least six months, you can also be on the electoral roll.

The people on the electoral roll are the ones who elect the **churchwardens** and members of the **PCC**. If you want to be one of these, you need to be on the electoral roll. All parish churches should have an electoral roll officer who makes sure that the roll is kept up to date.

(see **church organization**)

evangelical

Someone who is evangelical is committed to the good news of what **God** has done in **Jesus**. They want to share it with others.

When Evangelical has a capital 'E' it usually describes a person or **church** where the **Bible** is valued as a source of **authority** above anything else.

Name trail: the word 'evangelical' comes directly from the Greek word euangelion, *the word translated as 'good news' or 'gospel'.*

General Synod see **church organization**

hallowed

To hallow something means to make it **holy**. When in the Lord's Prayer we pray 'hallowed be your name', we are asking God that his name will be holy.
(see **holy** and **holiness**)

halo

A ring of light round a person's head is drawn to show that they are **holy**. **Jesus**, his **disciples** and **saints** are frequently shown with a halo round their heads – on **Christmas** cards, in stained-glass windows and other pictures. We might think it looks a bit silly, given that no one looks like this in real life. However, the artists are telling us something that is important: in the way they live, all these people reflect the light of **God**, which is normally unseen.
(see **holiness**)

liberal

Open-minded. Tolerant. Open to new ideas and ways of doing things. The word used to describe a very open Christian attitude to life. On issues that the Christian **Church** finds it difficult to agree – like the **ministry** of women or of people who are homosexual – a liberal would be likely to be accepting. (For the opposite, see **conservative**.)

Oxford Movement

At the time of the **Reformation**, there was a deliberate decision in the Church of England to steer clear of anything that was associated with the Roman Catholic Church. About 300 years later, in the 1830s, some of the leaders in the Church of England began to rediscover the value of some of these things, and sought to bring them back into church life. One of the key people was John Henry Newman. As he was based in Oxford, it became known as the Oxford Movement.

Quite a lot of things that are now taken as a normal part of church life stem from this movement. For example, celebrating **Holy Communion** as the main Sunday service, and using **candles** in **church** as a reminder of the light of **Christ**.

parish see church organization

paschal

Something to do with **Easter** can be described as paschal. Churches often have a paschal **candle** – the light is a symbol of the new life of the risen **Jesus**. Sometimes the Easter services are called 'paschal mysteries'. Paul calls Jesus 'our paschal **lamb**' (*1 Corinthians 5.7*).

The word reminds us that Christianity is rooted in Judaism. It means Passover – the time when Moses and Aaron led the Israelites on the start of their long journey out of Egypt and away from slavery.

Name trail: 'Passover' in Hebrew is pesach. *In Greek this became* pascha, *which gives us our English word 'paschal'.*

PCC see parish, in church organization

province see church organization

Reformation

A short name for big changes that happened in the 1500s, which had long-lasting effects. Before the Reformation the **Church** across Europe was **Catholic**, and governed by the Pope in Rome. However, lots of different people were beginning to question the way things were. Some of the key people were:

- Erasmus of Rotterdam (*c.*1467–1536, Holland)
- Martin Luther (1483–1546, Germany)
- Huldrych Zwingli (1484–1531, Switzerland)
- Thomas Cranmer (1489–1556, England)
- John Calvin (1509–64, France and Switzerland).

As well as people challenging ideas about theology, the English king, Henry VIII, challenged the **authority** of the Pope. He reigned from 1509 to 1547, and wanted to be divorced from his first wife. He needed permission from the Pope, who would not allow it. In the end, Henry broke off England's agreement that the popes ruled over the Church in England, and declared himself to be its head (which meant he could give permission for his own divorce).

Some of the other main changes that eventually took place in England were:

- services were in English not Latin;
- **Bibles** were printed in English and were available for people to read for themselves;
- **clergy** were better educated;
- the first English **prayer** book was published (in 1549). This became known as the Book of Common Prayer (or BCP for short).

This marks the beginning of the Church of England. The Lutheran Church is based on the ideas of Martin Luther. The Baptist Church roots much of its theology in the work of Zwingli. The Presbyterian and United Reformed Churches draw on the work of Calvin.

sacred

Another word for 'holy' – set apart for **God**.

tithe

'A tithe' is a tenth of something.

'To tithe' means to give a tenth of something to **God**. In the past, people might have paid a tenth of their crops to support the local **church**, abbey or monastery.

Name trail: 'tithe' comes from the word that means 'tenth' in Old English.

tradition

Something that has been handed on, with little change, over a long period of time. For example, what we do in **church** at **Holy Communion** or **baptism** is very like what the Church did from its earliest days. (See what Paul writes about 'the Lord's Supper' to people at the church in Corinth, in *1 Corinthians 11.23–26.*)

The three things that the Anglican Church holds together when it is thinking through issues are **Scripture**, tradition and reason. We look at what is in the **Bible**, what the Church has done from its earliest times, and apply our God-given minds to consider it all.

other stuff

'. . . the whole of life matters to God. What happens in church has to connect with the realities of life when we are not there. Christian faith permeates the whole of our lives.'

9

some more things to think about

alcohol

Noah got drunk (a bit embarrassing). **Jesus** turned lots of water into *lots* of **wine** (fantastic!). Paul thought Timothy needed a 'pick-me-up', so advised him to take a little wine (probably quite sensible). (See *Genesis 9.20–28*; *John 2.1–11*; and *1 Timothy 5.23*).

There's nothing wrong with alcohol in itself. It's what we do with it that matters. A drink with **friends** can be great. Too much can be not very nice.

Sometimes we can hide behind alcohol. We can use it to give us courage, or stop us thinking about something. But if we are doing this, it may mean there's a deeper problem to be faced. In the end, it's the Spirit of **God** not the spirit in the bottle that frees us to be true to ourselves. As Paul reminded the Christians in Corinth, 'Now the Lord is the Spirit, and where the Spirit of the Lord is, there is freedom' (*2 Corinthians 3.17*).

authority

Authority is not a very exciting word. It is about a person or institution having power and control over others. We might not like the sound of that, but there are two things to remember:

- it is a natural part of human relationships;
- exercised in the best possible way, authority is liberating and enables people to flourish.

The reason why parents and teachers have authority over their children and pupils is because there are certain duties they have to do: parents have to look after their children, helping them grow up to be good people; teachers have the task of helping pupils to learn.

People in authority have jobs to do, and if they do them well they will be loved and respected. If they don't, and they use their position of authority wrongly, then they will lose respect.

Paul has a guiding principle for anyone in authority: 'Do nothing from selfish ambition or conceit, but in humility regard others as better than yourselves. Let each of you look not to your own interests, but to the interests of others' (*Philippians 2.3–4*).

belonging

There are all sorts of things we might belong to: family, school, sports club, band, choir, football team or supporters club, and lots more. Belonging to something can give us the feeling of being loved and valued, needed and wanted.

Sometimes we choose what to belong to. Sometimes it chooses us. Maybe we have to wait to join something; or perhaps we want to stop being part of it.

Church is about belonging. It's about everyone being welcome. It might seem that the other people there have nothing in common with us – though if we scratch the surface we might be surprised. **God** created us to be people who belong – to each other and to him. If church doesn't reflect that, then we've got a bit of work to do.

(see **Trinity**)

body

The writer of Genesis 2 imagines **God** moulding the first man from the dust of the earth, just like a potter carefully shaping clay to make something beautiful. God's finishing touch is to breathe into this being his very own breath of life (*Genesis 2.7*). The risen

Jesus repeats this action, breathing onto his fearful **disciples** the life-giving breath of his Spirit (*John 20.22*).

We are so much more than just machines. This thing made up of so many different parts is a person, made in the image of God (*Genesis 1.27*). We are created to reflect something of God to whoever is looking – just as the image in the mirror shows us something of ourselves.

What we do with our body matters. We can help or hinder how we reflect God to those around us. When Paul was explaining this to **friends** in Corinth, he reminded them of this: 'your body is a temple of the **Holy Spirit** within you' (*1 Corinthians 6.19*). The human body is one of the most amazing, intricate, complex and beautiful things on the planet – and that means *you*.

call

When we call someone, we raise our voice to catch their attention over a distance. We might also mean that we telephone them. Christians often talk about being called by **God** to some particular task or **ministry**, but it is rarely as straightforward as hearing a raised voice or picking up the phone.

God had to get Moses' attention by making a bush burn (*Exodus 3.1–6*) – and even then Moses argued with God about what he was being asked to do. Isaiah got a vision (*Isaiah 6.1–8*). Paul got a blinding light and heavenly voice (*Acts 9.1–9*).

For us it is often much more mundane. Something a person says to us. A growing conviction inside us. Something that comes to us when we pray. Something that strikes us when we read the **Bible**. A call from God is often about lot of things coming together over time. God is persistent – he doesn't give up!

clothes/make-up

Some of us love dressing up; some of us hate it. But even if we normally prefer a pair of jeans and baggy top, we might wear something smarter for a **wedding**. There are two important things about clothes.

1 They are matched to particular occasions and activities. You probably wouldn't go to a wedding in the wellies and torn jeans you wear on the farm, or go climbing in your new stilettos.

2 They say something about who we are. When children play at dressing up they pretend to be someone else or explore a different role. We may not admit it, but most of us go on doing this as adults. We try out a different look and see if it suits us. What about you? Do you dress to hide yourself, or to express who you are?

It's the same with make-up. Enhancing what is already there is fine. Creating 'a look' as if for playing a part on stage is rather different. And if we are only accepted into a group when we are made up, then it doesn't say much for our **friends**.

Being happy with how we look is very closely linked to being happy with the person **God** made us to be.

death

I am looking at a slice of tree trunk, standing up on its edge. In the middle is cut out the shape of a cross. While the rings of wood are dark, the shape of the cross lets the light through. My eyes are drawn to the light falling on the table behind.

This is a Christian picture of death. Death is as real as this piece of wood is real. That this was once a living tree is a reminder that death is part of our created nature. We will all die, as will the rest of the created world.

When and how death happens does of course make a big difference to how we live with it. Whether it is facing our own death or the death of other people, we have to cope with the emotional pain of loss, absence and finality. There is no going back. There may be a sense of waste or pointlessness. While sometimes death is timely, there are other times when we are simply left with the unanswerable question, 'why?'

In **Jesus, God** was immersed in human life – up to and including death. His life was cut short by the violence of others. He saw it coming. His **friends** saw the end of all their hopes. Yet what they went on to see was new life; a demonstration that the life of God is bigger than what we see now. As with the tree trunk, we are led through the cross to the light beyond.

(see **resurrection, funeral**)

decisions

What shall I eat? What shall I wear? Shall I go out this evening? We have to make decisions about things all the time, every day. Many decisions are easy, not needing much thought. Some decisions are more difficult. What shall I do with my life? Which subjects should I choose? Should I stay on at school or go to college? Should I take this job? Shall I ask this person out? Shall I keep this bit in the book or cut it out?

How do we decide? **God** has given us brains. God has given us **friends**. God has given us the **Bible**.

(see **guidance**)

discipline

Discipline sounds negative. It means rules, being told what we can't do. It sounds like the opposite of fun.

In fact, discipline is about gaining something. A small child is restrained from running about freely because he needs to learn what is dangerous, and how to keep safe from things that harm. Over time the child learns, gains the trust of other people, and eventually, greater freedom.

An athlete agrees to the discipline of training. She pushes herself to go that bit further or faster. She mustn't eat certain things, and must exercise in a particular way. All of this is about being able to achieve something more.

Love involves discipline. If you love someone, you won't want to watch them hurt themselves. You will want them to make the best of their gifts. When **God** tells the Christians in Laodicea 'I reprove and discipline those whom I love' (*Revelation 3.19*), it is not about him wagging a disapproving finger. God wants the best for us. As the next verse goes on to show, God's discipline is just part of allowing God in – and enjoying the company.

doubt

Doubt is a really important part of **faith**. It is about not knowing all the answers and not being afraid to ask questions.

Sometimes doubts can seem to outweigh faith. Doubt begins to bite hard when our experience seems to go against what we thought we believed. **Suffering** and hardship make us ask, 'How can I believe that **God** loves me when *this* happens?'

Doubt comes and goes. Being a Christian does not mean being certain about God all the time. Sometimes it is more like hanging on by a thread, or feeling my way in the dark. Perhaps I can't see God, but God sees me, loves me and hangs on to me – with all my doubts. (see **suffering, faith**)

drugs

When the Israelites had escaped from Egypt and finally came to Mount Sinai, Moses went up the mountain to meet with **God**. The Israelites got fed up with waiting for him to come down and tell them what God was saying. They wanted something more immediate. They got Aaron to make them a calf out of their gold jewellery – and they worshipped this instead.

There was no life in that calf. It could do nothing for them. It was an excuse for a party, then the appalling consequences of their actions struck home (see *Exodus 32*).

Comparing recreational drug use is to this may seem a bit weird, but:

- like the golden calf, drugs distort our perception of reality;
- they too can offer a momentary high, which gives way to much more far-reaching damage;
- drugs can lead us into debt as we become more dependent on them – just as making the calf took all the people's gold;
- like the calf, drugs can dull our awareness of the life-giving presence of God;
- maybe there were some people there who were not sure that this was right, but got swept along by the peer pressure.

We don't need drugs to live a happy and fulfilled life. We might be drawn into taking them because we are struggling to manage a sense of hurt or pain. But drugs won't help, any more than the lifeless calf had anything to offer. It means we are looking in the wrong place.

Jesus told the Samaritan woman that what he had to offer was like 'a spring of water gushing up to eternal life' (*John 4.14*). Later he says, 'I came that they may have life, and have it abundantly' (*John 10.10*). There's nothing easy about changing direction, but there's both welcome and compassion in the one who calls us into fullness of life.

faith

Trust. Believing something to be true.

Daily life is full of acts of faith. I trust that when I turn on a tap, water will come out. I set an alarm on my mobile phone because I believe that it will remind me to go out when it goes off. I believe that you will meet me at the place and time we've agreed, because what I know about you makes me believe I can trust you.

I have faith in **God**. What I know about God makes me believe I can trust him. I look at the evidence of the biblical writers. I look at the words and acts of **Jesus**, his **death** and **resurrection**. I look at the evidence of the first Christians and the growing **church**. I think about the fact that it has lasted for over 2,000 years. I think of the billions of Christian believers around the world, and those who have been willing to die for their faith.

. Having faith isn't always easy. At times it gets knocked about by life's events. But we are not Christians alone. When believing is tough, we can rest on the faith of others.
(see **doubt**)

fame

I have won several Oscars, walked the red carpet, scored many winning goals, won lots of competitions, performed countless rescues single-handedly, fought off lots of baddies, and have generally been acclaimed as a hero – although *only* in my daydreams which I *never* told anybody.

At some point in our lives, most of us have dreamed of being famous. It's great to be noticed and to have our abilities recognized. It has a downside too, though. A famous person can be seen as public property, as 'a celebrity'. Every word and action is scrutinized. It can be hard just to be yourself.

If fame comes as a by-product of you being true to yourself, that's fine – though even that could be difficult to manage. If you go looking for fame for its own sake, then you may find that you are in danger of losing your sense of self. Fame is fickle. When the moment of celebrity has passed and the cameras have moved on to someone else, who are you then?

feelings

I have a favourite Greek word: *splanchnizomai*. It is as hard to translate as it is to pronounce. We find it in Mark 1.41 when **Jesus** cleanses the leper. It is translated 'moved with pity' – or compassion, or anger. The problem is, English doesn't really have a word to describe the gut-wrenching, stomach-churning feeling that *splanchnizomai* conveys. Whatever it was that Jesus felt when he heard the man's plea for help, it was powerful and got him in the guts.

Having powerful feelings is part of being human. It's the way God made us. The psalms are full of voices telling God how they feel, whether it's praise or complaint. The **prophet**s come close to that gut-wrenching feeling when they express the entwined anger and love of God for his people.

Whether it is the crying out of the leper or Jesus' gut-wrenching response, we are reminded of this: God's love for the whole of a person means that our feelings can be part of his purposes for us too.

friends

'It is not good that the man should be alone' (*Genesis 2.18*). So said God, and got on with the business of making sure the man would not be lonely. The animals were great, but he saw that human companionship was needed – and so it is. Many of us get on well with lots of people, but still have one or two whom we count as close friends.

True friendship is a wonderful thing. Friends trust each other, can listen and talk to each other, support and help each other, and enjoy each other's company. It is also risky. Friends are not perfect, any more than we are. When **Jesus** needed his friends to stay with him they fell asleep. When you think they might have stuck by him, they ran away (*Mark 14.32–50*). Yet Jesus turned up for them. That breakfast by the lake demonstrates that in true friendship there is always a place for forgiveness and restoration (see *John 21*).

gifts

Some gifts are obvious. We can see that someone is gifted at sport or music or public speaking or acting. Some people make us groan because they just seem to be good at everything. Schools identify those who are 'gifted and talented' at particular things.

More hidden gifts are just as important, though. Some people have a great gift of being able to offer friendship or hospitality to others. They might have a gift of generosity, kindness or making fantastic cakes.

There are two things to remember about gifts.

1 A gift is something given, and so it must have been given by someone. That someone is **God** (see *1 Corinthians 7.7*).
2 A gift is no good if it sits on a shelf in its wrapping. It has to be taken out and used. It's God's way of making the world more beautiful.

guidance

Joseph had his dreams (*Genesis 37*). Belshazzar got writing on the wall (*Daniel 5*). Paul had a vision of someone asking for help (*Acts 16*). Wouldn't it be nice, just sometimes, to have a sense of what direction **God** would like us to go in?

Christians often talk about God guiding them, or about God having a plan for their life. Others would say that if he has a plan, why does he not give us a map? A satnav would be great, but even a signpost to show we are on the right path would help.

The bottom line is that Christians do believe that God guides us. But although occasionally there is something very clear and strong, more often it will feel like a nudge from behind rather than a clear call from the front. Allowing God to guide us is about praying, reading the **Bible** and listening out for God in other people and circumstances. It can be hard to get away from the feeling that it is down to *me* to *do* something. Being truly open to God, and really patient, is difficult.

In the end it is about faithfulness and trust. Sometimes it's as if God says, 'You jump – I will be there to catch you.'
(see **decisions, listening, prayer**)

Hallowe'en

Here are a few facts.

- This popular celebration has a Christian name. It is a shortening of 'All-hallows-eve'. 'Hallows' means '**holy** ones' or '**saints**'. Therefore, Hallowe'en means 'the evening before All Saints' Day'. This is the day on which the **Church** celebrates the lives and faithfulness of all the saints – not just the ones who are remembered on their own special days. As All Saints' Day is celebrated on 1 November, Hallowe'en is 31 October.
- The things people do at Hallowe'en are to do with the belief that the spirits of the dead are out and about on that particular night. Dressing up with scary masks is to do with finding a disguise that will scare off any spirit who happens to be looking for me!
- These practices probably come from a mixture of different things – pre-Christian Celtic and Roman beliefs, and medieval Catholic ideas about **souls** having not yet got to **heaven**.

It's a great time for being creative and getting together with other people to celebrate – but to celebrate what? Some take the view that it is simply a commercial opportunity. Scary masks, costumes for witches, wizards, ghosts and skeletons are all on sale alongside pumpkins and toffee apples. There is also a concern that the focus on **death** and fear makes people vulnerable to exploitation by evil, and all that goes against **God**.

In the eighth century, Pope Gregory III moved the feast of All Saints from May to 1 November. He got the approach to Hallowe'en about right – he recognized that people need to face issues about death and what happens next, yet he wanted to emphasize that God is a God of life and of love, not a god of fear. The **resurrection** of **Jesus**, at the heart of Christian **faith**, shows that it is life and not death that has the final say.

holiness

We are used to seeing pictures of **saints** with a **halo** round their heads. They usually look pious, prayerful and **holy**. There are two immediate problems with the idea of holiness:

1 it sounds impossible;
2 it sounds very dull and **boring**.

We could list all sorts of things that we think holy people do and don't do. That probably wouldn't help our sense of it being rather a boring way of living.

Jesus painted a different picture: what you do is secondary; it's where you start from that matters. He tells his **disciples** that it's like a vine: he is the stem and they are the branches. If their starting point is being joined to him, then they will produce loads of grapes (see *John 15.1–17*).

Holiness is less about dos and don'ts, and more about trying to stay close to **God**. If that's the case, then the life of God will shine out.

Maybe the artists who depicted people with halos were on to something after all.

(see **saints**)

homosexuality

This might not seem like the most important issue in the world, but the **Church** certainly makes a lot of noise about it. It boils down to a question of how we approach the **Bible**. One of the ways Christians work things out is by looking to the literature of the Bible for clarity. This is *not* about treating it as an instruction book for how to live – it will tell us nothing about nuclear power or internet use, for example. It is more about looking to how it depicts the relationship of human beings with **God** and the created world. Homosexuality is referred to but not addressed in itself. So these are some of the issues.

- For a long time the Church – along with the rest of the world – believed that homosexuality was something people chose. As a lifestyle choice it was considered to be a deliberate wrong.
- Nowadays, very many more people recognize that homosexuality is not something a person has chosen; it is the way they are as God's beloved child.
- Some Christians still want to say that being in a sexually active homosexual relationship is wrong, because that is what they understand the Bible to be saying.
- However, there are letters in the New Testament that appear to accept slavery for example, which we would never do now. People abuse the Bible by not paying attention to the cultures and times when its literature was written.
- Christians believe that sexual activity belongs to a faithful, long-term, loving, committed partnership between two people. We might find it challenging that this applies to homosexual partnerships too. But surely we should affirm these values whether they are found in a homosexual or a heterosexual relationship. The Bible has far more to say about unfaithfulness and idolatry than about sexuality.
- At the heart of Christian **faith** is the belief that in giving God space in our lives, we are enabled to be more fully our true selves. If that means accepting homosexuality as part of my nature, it is vital that my Christian companions in the Church accept it too.

identity

A sense of who I am. What makes me 'me'.

We get this sense of self in different ways:

- maybe through relationships: I am someone's sister or brother, son or daughter, cousin or grandchild;

- maybe through being like, or wanting to be like, someone famous: that particular footballer or singer or TV personality;
- maybe through how we dress – a particular look or designer.

Sometimes other people look at us and label us: you are a goth, a geek, a chav, or an old fogey.

When you are on your own, in your own room with the door shut, who are you then? When you get undressed and go to bed, are you still the same person, and happy with yourself? Can you join in with what the psalmist says to **God**, 'For it was you who formed my inward parts; you knit me together in my mother's womb. I praise you, for I am fearfully and wonderfully made' (*Psalm 139.13–14*)?

(see **fame**)

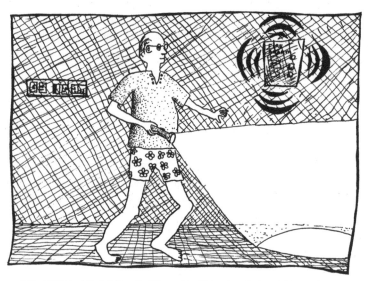

AS THE VICAR GOT UP TO TURN OFF THE
FIRE ALARM HE SUDDENLY REALISED THAT
HE WAS NOT WEARING HIS DOG COLLAR

internet

Brilliant invention!

Whether it's shopping, research, information-sharing, problem-solving, advice for mending things, information about times, places and people, keeping in touch across vast distances – it's all there, available at the touch of a button (assuming of course that you have a power source). How did we ever manage without it?

For something that has no physical reality, it's a good place to hide. Chatting online has no social context. No one needs to know who we really are, or if we really believe what we are saying. We can get away with things that we may never dare to say in someone's presence.

As with lots of brilliant inventions that have transformed human life, internet use calls for **wisdom**. When we meet Wisdom as a person in the book of Proverbs, she's right at the heart of what is going on. She was with **God** in the business of **creation**, and is at the centre of public discourse (Proverbs 1.20–21). She calls people to seek what is life-giving. 'For whoever finds me finds life . . . but those who miss me injure themselves' (*Proverbs 8, especially verses 35–36*). Whatever we use the internet for, Wisdom needs to walk with us in its cyber-streets.

marriage

Marriage is a bit like setting out on a journey – only without a map. You might know where you would like to go, how you would like to travel and where you'd like to pass through on the way; but you don't actually know what it will be like. In this respect it's a pretty odd kind of journey.

It is, of course, not putting details on the map that matters, but *who* you are travelling with. Marriage starts with love and commitment – to another person and the possibilities of life together. The promises made in marriage are about setting a framework within which we deal with the unexpected challenges that arise. It is also about a context where we can each grow as people. We have our spouse's best interests at heart, just as he or she has ours. When those things come into conflict, we work it out together.

Christians believe that the basis of all human relationships is the overflowing love of **God.** God's commitment to us is constant, faithful and forgiving. If the going gets tough, then the tough will look to God's love to top up our own.

morality

Morality is about what governs our behaviour. In many parts of the world where Christian **faith** has been prominent, Christian moral values are still held – even if attendance at **church** has declined.

Paul tells the church in Philippi that it boils down to this: 'Let each of you look not to your own interests, but to the interests of others. Let the same mind be in you that was in **Christ Jesus**' (*Philippians 2.4–5*) – and he goes on to describe the self-giving nature of Jesus seen in the **cross** and **resurrection**. Jesus himself spent a lot of time telling people that right behaviour had to go deeper than outwardly keeping the Ten Commandments. It was what was in the heart that mattered (e.g. *Matthew 5.21 onwards*).

Christians go on wrestling with difficult moral issues. It might seem odd to look back to documents that were written between two and three thousand years ago, when there is no mention there of things like fertility treatment, assisted dying, or chemical weapons. However, looking to the **Bible** is about finding a moral framework.

- What do we learn about the character of God?
- How is this seen in the life, **death** and resurrection of Jesus?
- What governs how the first Christians approached the issues that faced them?

As followers of Jesus, how do we act?

other faiths

There are lots of **religions**. There are differences that cannot be reconciled. There are different opinions about whether we all **worship** the same *God* really, or not.

There is no point in trying to water down our **faith** to something that all religious believers can accept. It can't be done. What can be done is to accept and respect our differences – and keep talking to one another.

religion

If someone describes a spiritual experience he or she has had, he or she might tell you:

- what happened;
- where it happened;
- what he or she saw/felt/heard;
- and might go on to say that he or she wants to keep remembering this, or enabling it to happen again.

All of these things are the basic elements of religion. It is about belief in **God**. The word 'religion' usually refers to a particular system of beliefs and practices – things that are done to enable people to go on being in touch with God.

Sometimes people have a very negative view of religion – as if it is just a list of things you have to do and believe in. If the **Church** feels like this, then perhaps it has lost its way. Religion is about the spiritual reality of friendship with God.

(see **spirituality**)

science

The word covers a vast range of ways in which we explore the physical reality of the world we live in. People have always engaged in scientific activity – it is part of human life to explore and use our knowledge to our advantage.

What is bizarre is the way in which science and **religion** are sometimes pitted against each other. Such a view seems to suggest that belief in **God** was only necessary in order to explain things we didn't understand. Now that we understand most things, we can dispense with the idea of God.

Christians don't always help. There is the great **creation** debate, for example: 'In Genesis 1 it says that God made the world in seven days, so the big bang can't be right – nor can evolution.' Oh dear . . .

- To start with, it is a mistake to read every verse of the **Bible** literally. Genesis 1 is no more a work of science than Joel 2.30–31 contains a weather forecast.
- Second, there are two creation accounts in Genesis, which are different from one another. Whoever compiled the book was not stupid in putting the two things side by side. What this tells us is that they were never understood as scientific accounts, but as saying very important things about God and about human beings.
- Third, the theory of evolution is an example of science opening up physical evidence that is wonderful, mind-blowing and that deeply enriches our understanding of God as **Creator**. These are not contradictory ideas, but complementary ones.

Scientific understanding is vital, enabling human beings to live well as good stewards of the created world.

sex

In the Yucatan Peninsula in Mexico, there are miles of underground rivers. Some people go to great lengths to explore them, or to swim in the underground *cenotes* (pools). Others simply enjoy the water when it appears at ground level – but it is the water running deep underground which sustains the pools visible at the surface.

It's the same with sex. Sometimes sex is treated as if it is merely an external quality. Someone looks 'sexy'. Sexual attraction is based on outward appearance. It's a frequent occurrence on film or TV that if two good-looking people meet, in no time at all they will be jumping into bed with each other. Blockbusters often prefer glamour over issues of safety and responsibility.

Sex is good, and fun. It is part of how **God** made us – so if we cut God out of the picture, we have a stunted view of what sex is. Far from seeming po-faced, Christians should be celebrating sex as a reflection of the self-giving love of God. In sexual intercourse, we make ourselves vulnerable in giving ourselves to another person. We forge an emotional connection, not just a physical one – and Christians believe that it is about a spiritually deep connection too.

That's why many christians hold on to the idea that sex belongs in **marriage**. It's too precious to treat casually. When we give ourselves sexually to another person we are exploring the deep wonderland of spiritual currents that is the whole of a human person, made in the image of the faithful and loving God.

spirituality

Spirituality is the life-blood of **religion**. It is about recognizing that we are more than bodies and minds. There is something about human life that is both part of and beyond ourselves.

Some people will describe themselves as being 'spiritual but not religious'. They have a genuine recognition of 'something more', yet do not identify that with a specific religious belief and practice.

Spirituality is about wholeness – something that **Jesus** brought to the lives of many people. The Samaritan woman set out to meet her physical needs, but at the well she found Jesus, offering 'a spring of water gushing up to eternal life'. This gushing water continues to flow and bring life in the Christian **faith** (*John 4.1–41*).

swearing

A small point, but **Jesus** makes it clear that we are not made dirty by things from the outside of us. Rather, it is what comes from the inside that matters (*Mark 7.14–15*). Words are powerful. They are to be used carefully and well.

vocation

A person's vocation is the thing that they feel they are called to do by **God**. A particular Christian **ministry** is often called a vocation – but so might be nursing, teaching, driving a taxi, or a multitude of other occupations. There are two things that need to come together in a vocation. First, it is a job that needs to be done, for some benefit in the world. Second, it is a job in which you are fulfilled and find pleasure. You might not enjoy absolutely every minute of it, but you feel that it fits you. If either of these bits is missing, then it might not be your vocation.
(see **call**)

Name trail: from the Latin word vocare, *which means 'to call'.*

Index of entries

absolution 58
acolyte 58
Advent 69
alb 58, 66
alcohol 91
almighty 3
altar 39
Anglican Church 80
APCM (Annual Parochial
  Church Meeting) 80
Apocrypha 80
apostle 24
archbishop 47
archdeacon 47
archdeaconry 80
area dean 47
Ascension 11
Ascension Day
  73–4
Ash Wednesday 71
atonement 11–12
authority 91–2

baptism 76–7
baptistery 39
belonging 92
Bible 12–13
bishop 48
blessing 24–5
body 92–3
Body of Christ 25
boring 80–1
bread 58–9

call 93
Candlemas 70
candles 40
canon 48
cassock 59, 66
cathedral 40
catholic 81
chalice 59
chancel 40–1
chapel 41
chaplain 48
chasuble 59, 66–7
choir 48–9
choruses 59
Christ 3
Christening 77
Christmas 13, 69
church 41–2, 49
church organization 82–3
churchmanship 81–2
churchwarden 50
clergy 50
clothes 93–4
colours 77
communion table 42
confession 59–60
confirmation 78
congregation 50
conservative 83
cope 60, 67
covenant 13
creation 14
Creator 3–4

Creed 60
cross 14, 42–3
crucifix 43
crucifixion 14–15
curate 51

deacon 51
dean 51
deanery 82, 84
death 94–5
decisions 95
denomination
  83–4
devil 25
diocese 82, 84
disciple 26
discipline 95–6
dog collar 84
doubt 96
drugs 96–7

Easter 15, 73
electoral roll 84
Emmanuel 4
Epiphany 69–70
eternal life 15
eternity 15
Eucharist 60
evangelical 84–5

faith 97–8
fame 98
fasting 26–7
Father 4
feelings 98–9
font 43
friends 99
funeral 78

General Synod 82, 85
gifts 99–100
glory 15–16
God 4–5
Good Friday 73
grace 16
guidance 100

hallowed 85
Hallowe'en 101
halo 85
heaven 16–17
hell 17
holiness 102
holy 5
Holy Communion
  60–1
Holy Spirit 5
Holy Week 72
homosexuality 102–3
hope 27
hymn 61–2

identity 103–4
Immanuel 5
incarnation 17–18
incense 62
incumbent 51
internet 105

Jesus 5
judgement 18

King 6

laity 51–2
Lamb 6
lay person 51–2

lectern 43–4
Lent 71–2
liberal 85
listening 27–8
liturgy 62
Lord's Supper 63

make-up 93
marriage 105–6
martyr 28
Mass 63
Maundy Thursday 73
mercy 18–19
messiah 7
minister 52
ministry 52
miracles 19
mitre 63, 67
morality 106
music 63

nativity 19
nave 24

omnipotent 7
omniscient 7
ordination 79
other faiths 107
Oxford Movement
   86

Palm Sunday 72
parable 28–9
parish 82, 86
paschal 86
Passiontide 72
pastor 52–3
paten 63

PCC (Parochial Church Council)
   86
penance 29
penitence, penitent 29
Pentecost 74
pew 44
prayer 29–30
prayers 63–4
preacher 53
Presentation 70
priest 53
procession 64
prophet, prophecy 30
province 82, 86
pulpit 45

Reader 54
rector 54
Redeemer 8
Reformation 87
religion 107
repent, repentance 30
requiem 79
resurrection 20
revere, reverent 31
righteousness 20–1
rural dean 55

sacrament 21
sacred 88
sacrifice 21–2
saint 31
salvation 22
sanctuary 45
Satan 31–2
Saviour 8
scarf 65, 67
science 107–8

Index of entries

Scripture 22–3
second coming 23
sermon 65
server 55
sex 108–9
shrine 45–6
Shrove Tuesday 70–1
sidesman/sideswoman/sidesperson 55
sin 32–3
soul 33–4
spiritual gifts 33–4
spirituality 109
steadfast 8
stole 67
suffering 34
surplice 67–8
swearing 109–10

tithe 88
tradition 88
Transfiguration 75
Trinity 8–9
Trinity Sunday 74–5

verger/virger 55–6
vestments 65–8
vestry 46
vicar 56–7
vocation 110

wedding 79
Whitsun 74
wine 68
wisdom 9–10
Word 10
worship 68
wrath 34–5

ND - #0058 - 270325 - C0 - 198/129/8 - PB - 9780281070213 - Gloss Lamination